PERFECT FRENCH IN 23 STEPS

Mary Dell

ISBN: 978-619-91591-2-5

CONTENTS

INTRODUCTION

GOOD NEWS ☺ French is actually easier than we sometimes think! Its grammar and pronunciation are often said to be very difficult but is this really true?

While there are indeed some difficult grammar elements, others are easier than in English.

Comparison with English

<u>What is easier?</u>

1. **Pronunciation**

That might sound surprising but the pronunciation in French has **<u>strict rules</u>** with very few exceptions and once you learn the rules, you can read and pronounce correctly any word. There are, of course, some difficult sounds which do not exist in English and it would surely take time to achieve perfection, but keeping a little foreign accent will not prevent you from speaking good and fluent French, and might even sound cute. Learning the rules of pronunciation is still a far easier task for you than for someone who is trying to learn English and will never know why "read", "great", "head", "hear", "heart", "wear", "learn" are pronounced in a different way even though they all have the same combination of vowels "**ea**"! The famous English transcription was invented to help but it is rather complicated itself. There is no such thing in French and you just need to follow the rules.

2. **Verb tenses**

The system of verb tenses is much simpler than in English. No Present Continuous (I am doing), no Present Perfect (I have done), no Present Perfect Continuous (I have been doing), no Past Perfect Continuous (I had been doing). Questions and negative forms are easier to make, and there are only two auxiliary verbs.

3. **No phrasal verbs!**

English phrasal verbs which are so many and where small particles like "in", "on", "for", etc. change the meaning of the original verb are really difficult for those who try to learn English. Fortunately, that does not exist in French.

<u>What is more difficult?</u>

1. **Gender**
Nouns in French have a gender – **masculine** or **feminine**.

Although some rules determining the gender of a word exist, there are a lot of exceptions. The solution to the problem is to always write down and learn every new word together with its article: "une" (feminine) or "un" (masculine).

2. **Conjugation** of verbs
The verb forms vary a lot according to the person and the verb tense. For each person (I, you, he, we…) there is a different ending, and each verb tense has its typical endings. On the other hand, most verbs obey to strict rules and only a few are irregular.

3. **Pronouns**
Some personal pronouns have more forms than their equivalents in English. BUT again there are rules with no exceptions so you just need to retain them.

In addition to these main differences, you will find some more, like for example the agreement of adjectives with nouns in gender and number but all in all there is nothing scary.

You will find here all the French grammar, explained in a SIMPLE way, with a minimum of academic terms, just as I have been explaining it to my students of French for several years. It is illustrated by a lot of examples, dialogues and exercises. To make things easier for beginners, everything is translated into English, and you will also find some common vocabulary, organized by different topics like sport or food, for example.

The key to success is to learn the grammar rules, and to try to dive into a **French atmosphere** as much as possible through listening to songs, reading books and articles, watching films and videos. Watching short video clips with subtitles can be a great start, and then, after gaining some confidence, watching without subtitles.

I hope you will enjoy the book and will soon think to yourselves "Hm, French is actually a piece of cake!" ☺

UNIT 1

PRONUNCIATION

Before we start with the rules, an important note:

You will see in the examples below the particles **le, la, un, une** in front of each noun. They are the articles which indicate the gender of a noun. **Le /un** – masculine; **la/ une** – feminine. The sooner you get used to writing down every noun together with its article, the better, because it will help you learn more easily which gender the noun is. We will talk more about the articles in the next unit.

Alphabet

Aa [a] Bb [be] Cc [se] Dd [de] Ee [ə] Ff [ef] Gg [ʒe] Hh [aʃ] Ii [i] Jj [ʒi] Kk [ka] Ll [el] Mm [em] Nn [en] Oo [o] Pp [pe] Qq [kju] Rr [er] Ss [es] Tt [te] Uu [ju] Vv [ve] Ww [dubləve] Xx [iks] Yy [igrek] Zz [zed]

Word stress

Stress in French falls on the final syllable of the word. However, not every word in a sentence is stressed. The stress pattern is based on entire phrases (groups of words) and it is actually the final syllable in each phrase which takes a prominent stress. This rhythm is one of the reasons French is so beautiful and melodious.

Vowels

<u>A</u>

1. Pronounced a short [a], open and similar to the sound in "c<u>a</u>r", but <u>shorter</u>. Not like in "bag"!

> **un chat** – cat
> **un alphabet** – alphabet

"A" can have an accent but it does not change the pronunciation.

> **à** – to, for
> **une pâte** – pastry

2. In the combination **ai**

AI is pronounced [e], short and open, like in "n<u>e</u>st".

> **une m<u>ai</u>son** – house
> **f<u>ai</u>re** – to do, to make

3. In the combinations **au, eau**

AU, EAU are pronounced closed [o] like in "f<u>o</u>rk", BUT <u>shorter</u>. Not open like in "pot"!

> **aussi** – too
> **beau** – nice
> **un tableau** – painting

<u>E</u>

This vowel is probably the most complicated as it is pronounced in a different way depending on whether there is an accent placed on it or not.

1. **E** without an accent and at the end of a word, it is NOT pronounced! It is called "e muet" (silent "e"). Exceptions are the one-syllable words like *me, te, de*, etc. which we will see below.

> **une gar<u>e</u>** – station
> **un livr<u>e</u>** – book
> **ell<u>e</u>** – she

2. **é** – with an "accent aigu"

It is pronounced [e] like in "p<u>e</u>ncil", but more closed. The lips are very close as if you were smiling or you were preparing to say "eat". We can call it a "smiling" é ☺

> **une <u>é</u>motion** – emotion
> **une poupe<u>é</u>** – doll
> **excit<u>é</u>** – excited

3. **e** before **r** at the end of a word

Same pronunciation like **é** : short and closed "smiling" [e]

> **un dîn<u>er</u>** – dinner
> **regard<u>er</u>** – to look
> **parl<u>er</u>** – to speak

4. **è** – with an "accent grave" or **ê** with an "accent circonflexe"

Both are pronounced [e], short and open, like in "n<u>e</u>st".

> **une mère** – mother
> **un père** – father
> **un(e) élève** – pupil

5. Before two consonants

Same pronunciation like **è** : short, open [e]

> **cette** – this
> **mettre** – to put
> **un restaurant** – restaurant

6. In one-syllable words or in the first syllable before a consonant. You prepare to say [e] like in "p_e_ncil" but instead you say closed [o] like in "f_o_rk", just shorter [o]

> **je** – I
> **le** – the
> **de** – of
> **debout** – standing

This is a typical specific French sound which does not exist in English. A difficult one, we must admit.

The best way to get familiar to it is to **listen to French speech as much as possible,** and to practice saying it. Short video clips, films, radio programs, anything is useful.

> - The combination **EU** is pronounced the same way.
> **deux** – two
> **un feu** – fire
> **mieux** – better
> **peu** – little

7. The combinations **EUR, OEUR** are pronounced in a similar way like EU, but the sound is more <u>open</u>.

> **une fleur** – flower
> **un acteur** – actor
> **le beurre** – butter
> **une heure** – hour
> **jeune** – young

<u>I</u>

1. Pronounced [I] like in "k_i_ck" or "cr_y_stal"

> **une rivière** – river
> **stimuler** – stimulate
> - î avec "accent circonflexe" – same pronunciation
> **une île** – island

2. The combination **ill** is pronounced:

- [il] similar to "b<u>ill</u>" but with a softer "L", in the following words:
une ville – city, town
un village – village
mille – thousand
million – million
tranquille – calm

- in any other word – [i:] similar to "p<u>ea</u>nut"
une fille – girl, daughter
une famille – family
brillant – bright

3. The combination **aill** is pronounced [ai] like the letter "I" in the English alphabet:

travailler – to work
bailler – to yawn

<u>O</u>

1. Pronounced closed [o] like in "f<u>o</u>rk", BUT <u>shorter</u>, in the following cases. (Not open like in "hot"!)

- **o** at the end of a word
un stylo – pen
un vélo – bike
- **ô** avec "accent circonflexe"
rôtir – to roast
un hôtel – hotel

- in the combinations **AU, EAU**
un bateau – ship
jaune – yellow
une auto – car

2. Pronounced open [o] before two consonants
une pomme – apple
un homme – man
sonner – to ring

3. The combination **OI** is pronounced similar to [wɒ] in "<u>wa</u>ter"

> **un soir** – evening
> **une poire** – pear
> **un poids** – weight

4. The combination **OU** is pronounced similar to [u] in "g<u>oo</u>d"

> **jouer** – to play
> **où** – where
> **un poulet** – chicken

<u>U</u>

Pronounced [ju] like in "p<u>u</u>re"

> **truc** – trick, thing
> **tu** – you

<u>Nasal vowels</u>

The nasal vowels are produced when air passes through the noise as well as the mouth. The closest English sound is **-ing** : sing, reading, making, etc. In French the "n" is even more assimilated.

The combinations are **a, e, i, o, y** plus **n** or **m**:

> **1. an, am, en, em** = [a^n]
> **bl<u>an</u>c** – white
> **<u>am</u>bitieux** – ambitious
> **comm<u>ent</u>** – how
> **un ex<u>em</u>ple** – example

> **2. in, im, un, ien, aim, ain, ein** = [e^n]
> **un matin** – morning
> **impossible** – impossible
> **un** – one
> **un lien** – link
> **la faim** – hunger
> **un pain** – bread
> **une peinture** – painting

> **3. on, om** = [o^n]
> **bon** – good
> **une compagnie** – company

<u>Consonants</u>

C can be pronounced:

1. [s] like in "<u>s</u>ound" before **e**, **i**, **y**

> **ce** – this
> **un cinéma** – cinema
> **un cygne** – swan

2. [k] like in "<u>c</u>at" before **a**, **o**, **u**, or a consonant

> **un carnaval** – carnival
> **une conversation** – conversation
> **le cuivre** – copper
> **écrire** – to write

Ç ("c cédille") before a, o, u to pronounce [s] like in "sound"

> **ça** – this
> **un garçon** – boy

G can be pronounced:

1. [ʒ] like in "vi<u>s</u>ion" or "trea<u>s</u>ure" before **e**, **i**, **y**

> **génial** – great
> **une girafe** – giraffe
> **un gymnase** – gym

2. [g] like in "<u>g</u>ame" before **a**, **o**, **u**, or a consonant

> **un regard** – look, glance
> **un argument** – argument
> **une gomme** – rubber
> **grand** – big

GU = [g] like in "<u>g</u>ame" ("u" is not pronounced!)

> **une guerre** – war

J = [ʒ] like in "vi<u>s</u>ion"

> **un jardin** – garden
> **bonjour** – hello

<u>S</u> can be pronounced:

1. [s] like in "<u>s</u>ound" at the beginning of a word or before a consonant

> **sur** – on
> **une poste** – post office

2. [z] like in "<u>z</u>ebra" between two vowels

> **un pay<u>s</u>age** – landscape

3. at the end of a word is NOT pronounced

> **des livres** – books

Attention: The "s" in particles like **les, des, mes**, etc., is pronounced [z] before a word beginning with a vowel or "h muet". This is called "liaison" [lie'zoⁿ] The "liaison" is another reason French language is so melodic.

> **des‿amis** – friends

<u>SS</u> = [s] like in "<u>s</u>ound"

> **possible** – possible

<u>H</u> is <u>never</u> pronounced!

> **habile** – skilful

BUT there are two kinds of "**h**" at the beginning of a word:

> - h muet – "silent" h. As if there were no letter at all.

When the word before the "h muet" ends in a vowel, the vowel is ommitted and replaced by an apostrophe.

> **l'hôtel** – the hotel
> **l'hiver** – the winter

> - h aspiré – no apostrophe
> **le héros** – hero
> **la hauteur** – height

<u>X</u> can be pronounced:

1. [ks] like in "Re<u>x</u>" before a consonant

> **expliquer** – explain

2. [gz] like in "e<u>x</u>ample" between two vowels

> **exercices** – exercises

A **consonant** at the end of a word is usually NOT pronounced!
 un lit – bed
 prêt – ready
 un parquet – parquet floor
BUT: sometimes **R** at the end of a word IS pronounced:

 un acteur – actor
 pour – for
and there are some more exceptions like **hôtel** where the final "l" is pronounced.

CH = [ʃ] like in "**sh**are"

 chanter – sing

TCH = [tʃ] like in "**ch**air"

 tchèque – Czech

PH – [f] like in "**ph**oto"

 un phénomène – phenomenon

QU = [k] like in "**c**at" ("u" is NOT pronounced!)

 quatre – four

GN – a specific sound, very similar to the sound in "**oni**on"

You pronounce together this soft [n] and the vowel which comes after
 un rossignol – nightingale
 une araignée – spider
 mignon – cute
 une montagne – mountain

- **TION** – typical ending of a number of words, pronounced [sion]
 une conversation – conversation
 une nation – nation

ARTICLES

Articles can be:

1. articles **définis**   – **LE, L', LA, LES** (the)
2. articles **indéfinis** – **UN, UNE, DES** (a/an/some)
3. articles **partitifs** – **DU, DE L', DE LA, DES** (some/any)

LE, L', LA, LES
ARTICLES DÉFINIS

Each noun in French has a gender: **masculine** or **feminine**, and the article is different according to the gender.

Masculine: **le** or **l'**

    le livre – the book
    le garçon – the boy

If the noun begins with a vowel or an "h muet", the article is **l'**:

    l'emploi – the job
    l'homme – the man

Feminine: **la** or **l'**

    la langue – the language
    la fille – the girl

If the noun begins with a vowel, the article is **l'**:

    l'université – the university
    l'énergie – the energy

As **l'** can be used with both masculine and feminine nouns, it does not help us know what gender the noun is. So when you write down a new word beginning with a vowel or «h muet», you should put «un» (masculine) or «une» (feminine), the indefinite articles as they clearly indicate the gender.

un orchestre – an orchestra
un hôtel – a hotel
une orange – an orange

Plural: <u>les</u>

The plural form is only one. It does not depend on the gender.

les garçons – the boys
les filles – the girls

Pronounciation of <u>les</u>

Most of the time the "s" is **not** pronounced.

However, as we have already mentioned, it is pronounced [z] when the following word starts with a vowel or "h muet". This is the French "liaison".

les‿idées – the ideas
les‿exemples – the examples
les‿hôtels – the hotels

Attention!

The two prepositions «**à**» (to) and «**de**» (of) combine with <u>le</u> and <u>les</u> to form new articles:

à + le = **au**
à + les = **aux**
de + le = **du**
de + les = **des**

Je dois parler <u>**au**</u> professeur. I must talk to the teacher.

Je dois parler <u>**aux**</u> élèves. I must talk to the students.

La décision <u>**du**</u> parlement est bonne. The decision of the Parliament is good.

La décision <u>**des**</u> députés est bonne. The decision of the deputies is good.

<u>WHEN</u>
<u>DO WE USE THE DEFINITE ARTICLE?</u>

1. We **<u>know</u>** the thing (or the person).
Le chat est sous **la** table. The cat is under the table. (this is our cat, our table).

2. We have already **<u>mentioned</u>** the thing or the person.
J'ai regardé un film japonais hier soir. **Le** film était bon, mais trop long.

I watched a Japanese film on TV last night. The film was good but too long.

3. The object is **<u>unique.</u>**

> **Le** Soleil – the Sun
> **La** Lune – the Moon
> **La** Terre – the Earth
> **La** Reine – the Queen

4. In some expressions with **<u>aller</u>** – **to** go

> aller chez **le** dentiste – to go to the dentist
> aller à **la** banque – to go to the bank
> aller **au** cinéma – to go to the cinema (au = à + le)

5. In the expressions with **<u>jouer</u>** – to play

> jouer **du** piano – to play the piano (du = de + le)
> jouer **du** violon – to play the violin

6. With **<u>geographic</u>** terms

> - all countries (in English only some, in French all!)
> **Le** Royaume-Uni – The United Kingdom
> **Les** Etats-Unis – The United States of America
> **La** France – France
> **Le** Mexique – Mexico

- the **<u>mountains</u>**

> **les** Alpes – the Alps
> **les** Pyrénées – the Pyrenees

- the **rivers, seas, oceans**

> **la** Méditerranée – the Mediterranean
> **l'**Océan Atlantique – the Atlantic Ocean
> **la** Tamise – the Thames
> **la** Loire – the Loire

- the **cardinal** points

> **l'**est – the East ; **de** l'est – Eastern
> **l'**ouest – the West ; **de** l'ouest – Western
> **le** nord – the North ; **du** nord – Northern
> **le** sud – the South ; **du** sud – Southern

> **dans le** Sud de la France – in the South of France
> **sur la** côte est de l'Angleterre – on the East coast of England
> **au** nord de – north of
> **au** sud de – south of

7. With **newspapers**

> **Le** Monde
> **Le** Nouvel Observateur

8. Some **expressions**

> écouter **la** radio – listen to the radio
> regarder **la** télé – watch TV

9. Talking about things **in general**

Attention!

When the French talk about things in general, they use **le, la, l'** or **les**, in difference with English where in such cases there is no article!

Il aime **les** animaux. He loves animals.

L'huile d'olive est bonne pour la santé. Olive oil is good for your health.

La vie est belle. Life is beautiful.

Je préfère **le** rock à **la** musique classique. I prefer rock to classical music.

UN, UNE, DES
<u>ARTICLES INDÉFINIS</u>

Un /**une** correspond to «a/an» in English.

<u>**Masculine**</u>: <u>**un**</u>

    un stylo – a pen
    un sac – a bag

<u>**Feminine**</u>: <u>**une**</u>

    une table – a table
    une chaise – a chair

<u>**Plural**</u>: <u>**des**</u>

There is only one plural form and it does not depend on the gender. It corresponds to «some» in English.

    des femmes – (some) women
    des hommes – (some) men
    des étudiants – students (**s** in «des» pronounced [z]!)

WHEN
<u>DO WE USE THE INDEFINITE ARTICLE?</u>

1. When we are talking about something <u>**for the first time**</u>.

C'est **un** livre intéressant. This is an interesting book.

J'ai **un** stylo dans mon sac. I have a pen in my bag.

2. In the sense of **someone, some, any**.

Il y a **une** fille devant la maison. There is a girl in front of the house.
Il y a **des** tableaux sur le mur. There are some pictures on the wall.
Il n'y a **pas de** tableaux sur le mur. Ther are not any pictures on the wall.
Indefinite articles are used in much the same way as **a, some, any** in English BUT not with jobs:
Elle est dentiste. She is a dentist.
Il est professeur. He is a teacher.

Attention !

Un, **une**, **des** change to **de** or **d'** in a negative sentence!

Il y a un problème. There is a probem.

Il n'y a pas de problème. There is no problem.
« Pas d'problème ! » (contracted in informal speech)

Ils imposent des règles strictes. They impose strict rules.

Ils n'imposent pas de règles. They do not impose any rules.

DU, DE LA, DE L', DES
<u>ARTICLES PARTITIFS</u>

The «articles partitifs» are used with uncountable nouns.

The uncountable nouns are:

- food products, like **de l'eau** (water**)**, **du lait** (milk), **du sucre (**sugar).

- materials, like **du verre** (glass), **du papier** (paper), **de l'or** (gold).

- abstract nouns, like **des connaissances** (knowledge**)**, **de la chance** (luck).

Some common uncountable nouns in English are countable in French:

> advice – un conseil
> furniture – des meubles, un meuble
> jewellery – des bijoux, un bijou
> news – des nouvelles, une nouvelle
> information – des informations, des renseignements

The «Article partitif» expresses an undetermined quantity of something (a noun which we cannot count). It corresponds to «some» or no article in English.

Je vais acheter **du** vin et **de la** viande. I'm going to buy some wine and some meat.
Je vais mettre **du** miel dans le gâteau. I'm going to put some honey in the cake.

Du, de la, de l' change to **de** or **d'** in a negative sentence:
Il y a du cacao dans cette boîte. There is some cocoa in this box.
Il n'y pas de cacao dans cette boîte. There is not any cocoa in this box.

UNIT 3

NOUNS

GENDER

Nouns in French have a gender – **masculine** or **feminine**.

How to tell whether a noun is masculine or feminine?

It is not an easy question ☺

A general rule says that if a noun ends in «-e», then it is feminine: **la femme** – woman, **la mère** – mother, **la lampe** – lamp, etc. However, there are several exceptions, like for example, **le père** – father (masculine), so we cannot rely on this rule. In addition, several words which do not end in «-e» are feminine: **la peau** – skin, **la peur** – fear, etc.

There are some typical endings for each gender which can help you. HOWEVER, to be sure what the gender of a noun is, you should **always learn it together with its article – le/un** or **la/une**!

Typical **endings for masculine nouns**

- **ment**	le loge**ment**	apartment
- **isme**	le capital**isme**	capitalism
- **asme**	un enthousi**asme**	enthousiasm
- **in**	un pouss**in**	chick
- **ier**	un ouvr**ier**	worker
- **eau**	un bur**eau**	desk, office
- **oir**	un compt**oir**	counter
- **at**	le Sén**at**	the Senate
- **eu**	un **jeu**	game
- **ou**	un gen**ou**	knee

The days of the week, the months and the seasons are all masculine. We will talk about them a bit later.

The languages are also masculine – le français, l'anglais, l'espagnol, etc.

Typical **endings for feminine nouns**

- **té**	la fier**té**	pride
- **tion**	la conversa**tion**	conversation
- **ance**	la résist**ance**	strength
- **ence**	la différ**ence**	difference
- **ude**	la certit**ude**	certainty
- **ure**	la cult**ure**	culture
- **esse**	la jeun**esse**	youth
- **ie**	la fant**aisie**	fantasy
- **aille**	la bat**aille**	battle

The continents are feminine: l'Europe, l'Amerique, l'Asie... as well as most scientific disciplines: la chimie, la géographie, la philosophie (BUT **les** maths!)

A few nouns have different meaning depending on whether they are masculine or feminine:

un tour	walk **Le** Tour de France	**une** tour	tower **La** Tour Eiffel
un mode	method un mode d'emploi	**une** mode	fashion
un poste	job	**une** poste	post office

Professions

Job titles ending in «-e» refer to both men and women:

    un/une journaliste – journalist
    un/une interprète – interpreter
    un/une libraire – bookseller

With some other professions the ending changes in feminine.

- en	- enne	un music**ien**	une music**ienne**
- eur	- euse	un dans**eur**	une dans**euse**
- eur	- ice	un act**eur**	une act**rice**
- er	- ère	un ouvri**er**	une ouvri**ère**

Some nouns referring to people have two versions – masculine and feminine:

un ami	**une** amie	friend (male / female)
un voisin	**une** voisine	neighbour (male / female)
un époux	**une** épouse	husband / wife

The gender of nouns is a tricky subject, there is no doubt about this. Sometimes two words which look very similar are not the same gender, like **la boisson** (drink) et **le poison** (poison), for example. The only way to learn an unfamiliar word properly and to be sure about the gender is to write it down <u>together with its article</u>!

PLURAL

The plural of most nouns is formed by **adding an -s** to the singular. This -s is NOT pronounced! The singular and the plural forms of a noun sound the same way and in spoken French it is the article and the context which help us understand whether the word is singular or plural.

une maison	**des** maisons	house / houses
un professeur	**des** professeurs	teacher / teachers

Some nouns form their plural by adding an **-x**. These are nouns which end in:

    -au / -eau

un tuyau	**des** tuyaux	hose / hoses
un bateau	**des** bateaux	boat / boats

- **eu**

un cheveu	**des** cheveux	hair
un aveu	**des** aveux	confession

- **ou**

un bijou	**des** bijoux	jewel / jewels
un genou	**des** genoux	knee / knees
un chou	**des** choux	cabbage
un caillou	**des** cailloux	pebble / pebbles

Nouns which end in -**s**, -**x**, -**z**, do not change in plural

une souri**s**	**des** souri**s**	mouse / mice
un pri**x**	**des** pri**x**	price / prices
un ne**z**	**des** ne**z**	nose / noses

Some **irregular** nouns

un journal	**des** journ**aux**	newspaper / newspapers
un animal	**des** anim**aux**	animal / animals
un travail	**des** trav**aux**	work
un œil	**des** yeux	eye / eyes
un œuf	**des** œufs	egg / eggs

Attention to the pronunciation of «**des yeux**» and «**des œufs**»!

Plural of some compound nouns:

des grands-parents	grandparents
des pommes de terre	potatoes
des chefs-d'œuvre	masterpieces

UNIT 4
ÊTRE

The verb plays a central role in a sentence, therefore verb tenses and conjugation deserve special attention.

Verbs are always presented with their <u>infinitives</u>, just as in English. The difference is that they are single words without the additional particle « to ».

In French there are two main auxiliary verbs: **être** (to be) and **avoir** (to have). They can be full verbs (having their own meaning), and can also help as auxiliary verbs in the formation of some verb tenses.

Before we get started with the verb **être**, let's see the personal pronouns:

JE, TU, IL, ELLE…
<u>PERSONAL PRONOUNS</u>

je	I
tu, **Vous**	you (one person)
il	he / it
elle	she / it
nous	we
vous	you (plural)
ils/elles	they

The pronouns **il** and **elle** correspond to the gender of the noun that they replace, no matter if it refers to a person or to an object. There is no special pronoun similar to the English « it ».

Ma sœur est étudiante. My sister is a student.

Elle est étudiante. She is a student.

Cette table est trop petite. This table is too small.

Elle est trop petite. It is too small.

Ils (plural) – refers to a group of men only (or objects which are all masculine).

elles (plural) – to a group of women only (or objects which are all feminine). If the group is mixed, with at least one man, the pronoun will be **ils**.

J'ai trois sœurs et un frère. I have three sisters and one brother.

Ils sont tous plus âgés que moi. They are all older than me.

Tu and Vous

When you speak to one person, there are two options:

    - **tu** – familiar
Used when you speak to a family member, a friend, a close colleague.

    - **Vous** – polite and respectful
Used when you speak to a stranger, a new acquaintance, a business partner, a person older than you, etc.

Tom, **tu** n'es pas un bon garçon ! Tom, you are a naughty boy!

Miss Marple, **Vous** pouvez compter sur moi. Ms. Marple, you can rely on me.

On

On (a nasal sound !) is a special pronoun which can mean :

    - one/you /they – when we speak **in general**
On ne sait jamais. You never know. (in general)

    - we – commonly used in everyday speech to replace « nous »
On va regarder le football ce soir ? (= Nous allons regarder le football ce soir ?) Are we going to watch the football tonight ?

We can now begin studying the verb **être** in detail.

1. ÊTRE as a <u>full verb</u> – to BE

<u>Present</u>

<u>Affirmative</u>

je suis	I am
tu es / vous êtes	you are
il/elle est	he/she/it is
nous sommes	we are
ils/elles sont	they are

Vous êtes can be used either when you speak to one person (politely) or to several people.

Vous êtes très gentil, M. Holmes ! You are very kind, Mr. Holmes!

Vous êtes de très bons élèves. You are very good students.

(-) <u>Negative form</u>

ne...pas

The **two** particles – **ne** and **pas**, « frame » the verb.

Je **ne suis pas** espagnole, je suis française. I am not Spanish, I am French.

If the verb begins with a vowel, « **ne** » becomes « n' ».

Il **n'est pas** marié. He is not married.

The negative form is always the same with any verb and any verb tense, which is easier than in English (no don't, doesn't, didn't)

(?) <u>Question form</u>

The rules for making a question form are universal too, and valid for all verbs and verb tenses.

There are **three** ways to form a question:

1. « **Est-ce que** » at the beginning of a sentence:

Est-ce qu'il est allemand ? Is he German?

Est-ce que les enfants sont à l'école ? Are the children at school?

2. Intonation

Another easy way to make a question, is by using a rising intonation.

Il est allemand ? Is he German?

Tu es fatigué ? Are you tired?

Both ways are used in colloquial speech.

3. Inversion

An inversion is exchanging the places of the verb and the subject (who/which performs the action).

This way to make a question is relatively rare, but we can see it in one very common question:

Où es-tu ? Where are you?

If the sentence begins with a **question word**, like « Où » (where), it is followed by one of the three ways: **est-ce que**, **intonation** or **inversion**.

For example, « Why are you angry ? » :

Pourquoi tu es fâché ? (intonation)

Pourquoi est-ce que tu es fâché ? (« est-ce que »)

Pourquoi es-tu fâché ? (inversion) rarely used

(- ?) <u>Negative question</u>

Est-ce que tu n'es pas prêt ? Aren't you ready?

Possible answers :

Non, je ne suis pas prêt. No, I'm not.

Si, je suis prêt ! Yes, I am ready!

Attention ! « **Si** », not « oui », can be an answer to a negative question !

<u>So am I</u>

<u>Moi aussi</u>

- Je suis fatigué. I am tired.
- **Moi aussi**. So am I.

<u>Neither am I</u>

<u>Moi non plus</u>

- Je n'ai pas faim. I am not hungry.
- **Moi non plus**. (not Moi aussi). I'm not either.

<u>Question tags</u> (Are you? Aren't you? Is he? Isn't he?)

<u>N'est-ce pas ?</u>

Here again French is easier and simpler. In English the question tags vary a lot, while in French it is always « n'est-ce pas ».

Belle musique, **n'est-ce pas** ? Nice music, isn't it?

Tu es là tous les vendredis, **n'est-ce pas** ? You are here every Friday, aren't you?

The verb **être** takes part in many frequently used expressions.

Note that in the following expression, **être** is in <u>present</u> tense, not in past as in English:

Je suis né(e) – I was born.

Où est-ce que **tu es né** ? Where were you born?

EXPRESSIONS with ÊTRE

être fatigué	to be tired
être surpris	to be surprised
être au courant	to know
être en retard	to be late
être à la maison	to be at home
être au travail	to be at work
être sur le point de	to be about to
être d'accord avec	to agree with
être prêt à	to be ready to
être en vacances	to be on holiday

A classic question with **être** is:

Qu'est-ce que c'est ? What is this?

C'est... This is...

C'est le nouveau modèle iphone. This is the new iphone model.

C'est = ce est (the apostrophe replaces the « e », because the following word starts with a vowel)

Demonstrative adjectives

These adjectives are more complex than in English as they vary according to the gender.

ce / cet (masc.), **cette** (fem.)	this / that
ces	these / those

Ce/cet are both masculine, « cet » is used when the noun begins with a vowel or « h muet ».

Ce fromage est bon. This cheese is good.

Cet ouvrage est utile. This book is useful.

Cet homme est américain. That man is American.

Cette table n'est pas en bois. This table is not made of wood.

Ces livres sont en anglais. These books are in English.

USEFUL EXPRESSIONS WITH « C'EST »

C'est juste. That's right.

Ce n'est pas vrai. That's not true.

C'est assez. That's enough.

Qu'est-ce que c'est ? What's this? / What's that?

C'est bon. It is good.

C'est bon d'avoir beaucoup d'amis. It's good to have a lot of friends.

C'est pratique. It is convenient.

C'est pratique de voyager en bus. It is convenient to travel by bus.

C'est important. It is important.

C'est important de manger de la nourriture saine. It is important to eat healthy food.

C'est possible / impossible. It is possible/impossible.

C'est impossible de réussir sans travailler beaucoup. It is impossible to be successful without working hard.

C'est nécessaire. It is necessary.

Ce n'est pas nécessaire de demander un visa. It is not necessary to apply for a visa.

C'est facile. It is easy.; **C'est difficile.** It is difficult.

Ce n'est pas facile d'apprendre une langue étrangère. It is not easy to learn a foreign language.

C'est intéressant. It's interesting.

C'est magnifique. It's wonderful.

C'est super. That's great.

2. **ÊTRE** as an <u>auxilliary (helping) verb</u>

Être as an auxilliary verb helps in the formation of some verb tenses which we will study in detail further.

Je suis allé au travail à 9 heures. I went to work at 9am.

Here « je suis » does not mean « I am », it is just a helping verb.

The following exercises are in the form of dialogues, like all exercises in the book, as we would like to stay as close as possible to the real everyday language.

EXERCISES   **Complete the gaps:**

1. – Il … médecin, … ? He is a doctor, isn't he?

 - Non, il … dentiste. No, he is a dentist.

…

2. - Où … tu ? Where are you?

- Je … à Starbucks avec une amie. I'm in Starbucks with a friend of mine.

….

3. - Est-ce qu'ils … de l'Angleterre ? Are they from England?

- Non, ils … de l'Irlande. No, they are from Ireland.

….

4. - Est-ce que tu … fatigué ? Are you tired?

- Non, ça va. No, I'm not. I'm OK.

…

5. – Elle … mignonne, n'est-ce pas ? She is very cute, isn't she?

- Oui, elle … magnifique. Yes, she is gorgeous.

You can find a lot of Internet sites with exercises or tests to check your level and it is no doubt useful, but the best exercise is still to **read** and **listen** to French as much as possible – books, songs, video clips, films, TV and radio shows. The more, the better!

The following story (close to a real life story) illustrates the grammar rules.

DIALOGUE « Meeting a new friend in a bistrot »

Place of action: Paris, France

Characters:

Peter – American, software specialist, likes listening to hard rock, loves tennis

Olivier – Frenchman, football fan, likes going out at night, plays tennis in his free time

Julie – Frenchwoman, works for the same company as Peter, likes music, dance, good food

Kate – Peter's sister, student, interested in fashion, shopping, listens to latino and pop

Peter has been in Paris for a few months. He works for a big software company. One Friday, he meets a Frenchman in a « bistrot ».

Peter : Il fait trop chaud aujourd'hui, **n'est-ce pas** ?

Peter: It is very hot today, isn't it?

The Frenchman : Oui, **c'est** vrai… Heureusement qu'**on est** à la terrasse, il y a quand même un peu d'air qui rafraîchit !

The Frenchman: Yes, it is indeed. Good thing we are outside, there is a bit of fresh air!

Peter : Les terrasses parisiennes **sont** fantastiques ☺

Peter: Parisian « terrasses » are fantastic ☺

The Frenchman : Absolument. Elles ont un charme unique. Vous **n'êtes pas** français donc ?

The Frenchman: Absolutely. They have a special charm. So you are not French?

Peter : Non, **je suis** américain. Je m'appelle Peter.

Peter: No, I'm not. I am American. My name is Peter.

The Frenchman : Enchanté. Moi, **je suis** Olivier.

The Frenchman: Nice to meet you. I am Olivier.

Peter : Enchanté.

Peter: Nice to meet you too.

Olivier : **Tu es** là en vacances ?

Olivier: Are you here on holiday?

Peter : Non, pas en vacances. Je travaille ici, mais **je ne suis pas** encore habitué au mode de vie français. Ça fait à peine deux mois que je vis en France.

Olivier : Parfait, tu auras du temps pour tout apprendre. J'espère te revoir bientôt. Je viens ici tous les vendredis.

Olivier : Super ! A bientôt alors !

Peter: No, I'm not. I live and work here but I am not used to French lifestyle yet. I've only been in France for a few months.

Olivier: Cool! You'll have time to learn everything. Hope to see you again soon. I come here every Friday.

Peter: Great! See you soon then!

USEFUL VOCABULARY: to meet, to greet, to thank, to apologize

<u>**Meeting for the first time**</u> :

Enchanté !(de faire votre connaissance) Nice to meet you !

<u>**Greetings**</u> :

Bonjour ! Hello! / Good morning / Good afternoon!
Bonsoir ! Good evening!
Salut ! Hi! (informal)
Je suis heureux de te voir. Nice to see you.

Enchanté d'avoir fait votre connaissance. Nice meeting you.
Au revoir ! Goodbye!
Ciao ! Bye / Cheers! (informal)
Ravi de t'avoir vu ! Nice seeing you!
Saluez de ma part... Give my regards to…
Salue bien... (informal) Say Hello to...
A bientôt ! See you soon!
A demain ! See you tomorrow!
A lundi ! **A lundi prochain** ! See you on Monday! See you next Monday!
A tout à l'heure ! See you later!

Prends soin de toi ! Take care!
Bonne nuit ! Good night!
Dors bien ! Sleep well!

Fais de beaux rêves ! Sweet dreams!

Bonne journée ! / Bonne soirée ! Have a nice day/evening!

Answer : **Merci ! A toi aussi.** Thanks, same to you.

> **Bon voyage** ! Have a safe trip!
> **Bonne chance** ! Good luck!
> **Amuse-toi bien** ! Have a nice time!
> **Bon appétit** ! Enjoy your meal!
> **Meilleurs vœux** ! Best wishes!
> **Remets-toi vite** ! Get well soon!

Thanks :

> **Je te/vous suis très reconnaissant(e)** ! I'm very grateful to you!
> **Merci** ! Thank you!
> **Merci beaucoup** ! Thank you very much!
> Answer : **Je t'en prie / Je vous en prie** ! You are welcome!
> Other possible answers to « Thank you »:
> **Pas de problème.** No problem.
> **C'est bon. / De rien.** It's all right / Don't mention it.
> **C'était un plaisir pour moi.** My pleasure.
>
> **S'il te plaît, s'il vous plaît / je vous en prie.** Here you are.
> Answer: **Merci** ! Thank you!

Asking :

> **Est-ce que tu peux / vous pouvez me rendre service ?** Could you do me a favour?
> **S'il te plaît / S'il vous plaît** ! Please!

Apologies :

> **Je suis désolé.** I am sorry.
> **Je m'excuse.** I apologize.
> **Je vous prie d'accepter mes excuses** ! (formal) Please accept my apology!
> Answers :
> **Ça va.** It's all right.
> **Pas de soucis / Ne t'en fais pas / Pas de problème.** No worries / Don't worry / No problem.
> **C'est pas grave.** (informal) Not a big deal.
> **Pardonne-moi / Pardonnez-moi.** Please forgive me / I beg your pardon.
> **Ce n'était pas ma faute.** It wasn't my fault.
> **Ce n'est pas ce que je voulais dire.** I didn't mean it.
> **Ça n'a pas d'importance.** It doesn't matter.
> **C'est pas grave.** Never mind.
> **Désolé de te déranger / Désolé de vous déranger.** I'm sorry to bother you.

Excuse-moi ! Excusez-moi ! Excuse me!
- to attract attention (in a shop, for example)
- to pass by (in a crowded bus, for example)
Pardon ? Excuse me? / Pardon ? (when you have not understood)
You can add : **Vous pouvez répéter, s'il vous plaît ?** Could you repeat that please?
...
Santé ! Cheers!
A tes souhaits ! Bless you!
Félicitations ! Congratulations!
Bravo, bon travail ! Good job!
Bravo ! Good for you!
Dommage ! What a pity!

To agree and disagree :

Je pense / Il me semble. I think so.
Je suppose que tu as raison. I guess you are right.
Je ne pense pas. I don't think so.
J'espere. I hope so.
J'espère que non. I hope not.

How are you ?

Comment vas-tu ? / Comment ça va ? (informal) / **Comment allez-vous ?** (formal) How are you?
Ça va, merci. (informal) Fine, thanks.
Je vais bien, merci. I am very well, thank you.
Très bien, merci. Very well, thank you.
Et toi ? / Et vous ? How about you? And you?
Qu'est-ce qui se passe ? What's going on?
Quel est le problème ? Qu'est-ce qui se passe ? What's wrong? / What's the matter?

UNIT 5
AVOIR

1. AVOIR as a <u>full verb</u> – to HAVE

<u>Present</u>

Affirmative form

j'ai	I have
tu as, vous avez	you have
il / elle a	he / she / it has
nous avons	we have
ils / elles ont	they have

(-) Negative form

ne....pas

Je n'ai pas de voiture. I don't have a car.

Il n'a pas de voiture. He doesn't have a car.

(?) Question form

est-ce que / intonation / inversion

Est-ce que tu as une voiture ? Do you have a car?

Tu as une tablette ? Do you have a tablet?

(-?) <u>Negative question</u>

est-ce que / **intonation** and **ne…pas**

Est-ce que tu n'as pas de voiture ? Don't you have a car?

Tu n'as pas un laptop ? Don't you have a laptop ?

Moi aussi – Me too

Moi non plus – Neither have I.

…, **n'est-ce pas** ? – the universal question tag for all verbs and tenses

Tu as des livres français, **n'est-ce pas** ? You've got some French books, haven't you?

EXPRESSIONS with AVOIR

Curiously, several frequently used expressions with **AVOIR** match with English expressions with « to be ».

avoir chaud	to be hot
avoir froid	to be cold
avoir faim	to be hungry
avoir soif	to be thirsty
avoir sommeil	to be sleepy
avoir raison	to be right
avoir tort	to be wrong
avoir de la chance	to be lucky
avoir l'habitude	to be used to
avoir mal	it hurts
avoir envie	to want

2. AVOIR as an <u>auxilliary verb</u>

Avoir helps to form several verb tenses which we will study in detail further.

J'ai acheté le manuel hier. I bought the textbook yesterday.

Here « j'ai » does not mean « I have », it is just a helping verb.

DIALOGUE   **« About the beauty of France »**

At work. Peter is talking to a colleague about France.

Peter : Parle-moi un peu plus sur la France. Est-ce que tu es de Paris ?

Collègue : Oui, je suis de Paris, mais mes parents sont de Grenoble, et **j'ai** beaucoup de cousins là-bas. J'y vais souvent les voir.

Peter : **J'ai envie** d'aller en vacances quelque part. Tu peux me recommander un bel endroit en France ?

Collègue : Oh **nous avons** tellement de beaux endroits... Pour des vacances vraiment romantiques il n'y a pas mieux que Paris, mais tu y habites et tu le connais déjà. D'ailleurs, je peux te montrer quelques coins magnifiques cachés des foules de touristes. Une autre destination intéressante, c'est la Côte d'Azur – Nice, Cannes ou Saint-Tropez, beaucoup de soleil, ciel bleu et du bon rosé. Ou bien Biarritz, qui est sur la côte ouest, c'est aussi fabuleux. Si tu aimes la montagne, **on a** aussi des stations de ski fantastiques, Avoriaz en Haute Savoie, par exemple, ou une autre que je connais bien, parce qu'elle n'est pas loin de Grenoble – Autrans-Méaudre.

Peter: Tell me a bit more about France. Are you from Paris?

Colleague: Yes, I am. But my parents come from Grenoble, and I have a lot of cousins there so I often go to see them.

Peter: I would love to go on holiday somewhere in France. Can you recommend me a nice place?

Colleague: Oh we have so many beautiful places... For a really romantic holiday, there is nothing better than Paris, but you live here and you know it already. By the way, I can show you some lovely spots hidden from the crowds of tourists. Another perfect destination is la Cote d'Azur – Nice, Cannes or Saint-Tropez, a lot of sun, blue sky, some great rosé. Or Biarritz, which is on the west coast. They are all fabulous. If you like the mountains, we also have some fantastic ski resorts, Avoriaz en Haute Savoie, for example, and one I know well because it is not far away from Grenoble – Autrans-Méaudre.

Peter : Je me rappelle maintenant que j'ai vu un film français amusant, où quelques amis étaient allés faire du ski. Il y avait des paysages de montagne splendides dans ce film.

Collègue : Tu parles probablement du film « Les bronzés font du ski ». Oui, **nous avons** des montagnes magnifiques, et pas seulement pour faire du ski. L'été, c'est un paradis pour la randonnée. De longues routes dans les hautes montagnes, comme la Haute Randonnée Pyrénéenne, ou bien, des options moins lourdes, comme Le Parc Naturel Régional du Luberon avec ses petits villages pittoresques où tu peux goûter à la cuisine traditionnelle française, et du bon vin, bien sûr, encore la randonnée dans les Alpes Maritimes qui va de Menton à Marseille.

Peter : Wow ! Ça parait très attirant ! Mais tu viens de me donner beaucoup d'informations, je ne suis pas sûr d'avoir tout retenu.

Collègue : Tu sais quoi, **j'ai une idée**. Un de mes cousins à Grenoble travaille pour une agence touristique, il est compétent sur ce sujet. Tu peux parler avec lui, il va te faire le point sur les différentes opportunités pour de belles vacances en France.

Peter : Super ! Merci beaucoup !

Peter: Talking about mountains, I remember now a funny French movie about some friends who went skiing. There were amazing mountain views in this movie.

Colleague: You are probably talking about « Les bronzés font du ski ». Yes, we have wonderful mountains, and not only for skiing. Summer is a paradise for hiking. Long distance high mountain routes, like the Haute Randonnee Pyreneenne, or lighter options like Luberon Natural Regional Park with its picturesque small villages where you can taste traditional French cuisine, and good wine, of course. Or a Mediterranean trail which runs from Menton to Marseille.

Peter: Wow! That sounds so attractive! But you just gave me a lot of information, I am not sure I retained everything.

Colleague: You know what? I have an idea. One of my cousins in Grenoble works for a travel agency. He is very competent on this subject. You can talk to him and he will tell you everything about different opportunities for a nice holiday in France.

Peter : Great! Thank you very much!

USEFUL VOCABULARY : nationalities, family

Tu es d'où ? Where are you from?

les États-Unis – The United States of America; **Américain,e** – American

la France – France ; **français** – French ; **Français** – Frenchman
Française – Frenchwoman

l'Angleterre – England ; **anglais** – English ; **Anglais** – Englishman ; **Anglaise** – Englishwoman

la Grande-Bretagne – Great Britain ; **Britannique** – British

le Royaume-Uni = l'Angleterre, l'Ecosse, le Pays de Galles et l'Irlande du Nord.

The United Kingdom = England, Scotland, Wales and Northern Ireland

l'Ecosse – Scotland ; **Ecossais** – Scottish

le Pays de Galles – Wales ; **Gallois** – Welsh

l'Irlande – Ireland ; **irlandais** – Irish ; **Irlandais** – Irishman ; **Irlandaise** – Irishwoman

<u>Family – famille</u>

une mère – mother ; **une maman** – Mum
un père – father ; **un papa** – Dad
des parents – parents (same spelling, pronunciation completely different!)
un mari – husband ; **une femme** – wife ; **un époux / une épouse** – spouse
je suis né (e) à – I was born in
un(e) enfant – child ; **des enfants** – children ; **un(e) adulte** – adult
un bébé – baby ; **des jumeaux** – twins ; **un(e) adolescent(e)** – teenager
un fils – son ; **une fille** – daughter
une sœur – sister ; **un frère** – brother
une grand-mère – grandmother ; **une grand-maman** – grandma
un grand-père – grandfather ; **un grand-papa** – grandpa
des grands-parents – grand-parents
une tante – aunt ; **un oncle** – uncle ; **un neveu** – nephew ; **une nièce** – niece
un cousin / une cousine – cousin ; **un parrain** – Godfather ; **une marraine** – Godmother
une belle-mère – mother-in-law
un beau-père – father-in-law

All in-law family members are called **beau**/**belle** (which means handsome/beautiful) :
un beau-fils, une belle-fille, un beau-frère, une belle-sœur. Nice, isn't it? ☺

un ami / une amie – friend ; **un garçon** – boy ; **une fille** – girl
un petit ami / une petite amie – boyfriend / girlfriend
une relation – relationship
une amitié – friendship
être amoureux – to be in love with ;
tomber amoureux de – to fall in love with
sortir avec quelqu'un – to go out with
s'entendre bien avec – to get on well with
se fiancer – to get engaged
se marier – to get married
rompre – to split up with
se disputer – to argue with

Zodiac signs – Signes du Zodiaque

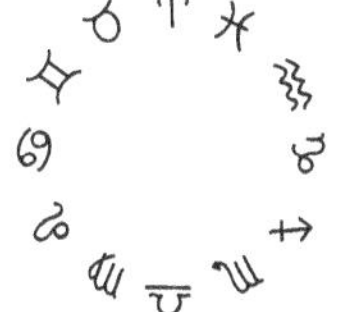

Verseau – Aquarius ; **Poissons** – Pisces ; **Bélier** – Aries ; **Taureau** – Taurus ; **Gémeaux** – Gemini ; **Cancer** – Cancer ; **Lion** – Leo ; **Vierge** – Virgo ; **Balance** – Libra ; **Scorpion** – Scorpio ; **Sagittaire** – Sagittarius ; **Capticorne** – Capricorn

If you are interested in the Zodiac, you can check your horoscope for the day on a French site. You can also watch video clips on Youtube where there are fascinating stories about stars, constellations, etc. Any source of information, as long as it is in French, is useful ☺

IL Y A
THERE IS / THERE ARE

There is only one form for both singular and plural so it is easier than in English.

Affirmative form

Il y a un frigo dans la cuisine. There is a fridge in the kitchen.

Il y a plusieurs placards dans la cuisine. There are a lot of cupboards in the kitchen.

(-) Negative form

ne...pas

Il n'y a pas de table dans la chambre. There is no table in the room.

Il n'y a pas de tableaux sur le mur. There aren't any pictures on the wall.

(?) Question form

est-ce que

Est-ce qu'il y a de la bière dans le frigo ? Is there any beer in the fridge?

Est-ce qu'il y a beaucoup de bistrots dans le centre ? Are there many pubs in the center?

(- ?) Negative question

est-ce que and **ne...pas**

Est-ce qu'il n'y a pas de billets pour le concert ? Aren't there any tickets for the concert?

COMPARISON between AVOIR and IL Y A

The difference between **Avoir** and **Il y a** is like the difference between « have » and « there is » in English.

Ils ont un chat. They have a cat.

Il y a un chat dans la rue. There is a cat in the street.

EXERCISES Complete the gaps:

1. – **Tu … un peu de temps ?** Have you got a minute?

- **Oui, j'en …, pourquoi ?** Yes, I have. Why?

…

2. - **Je… rendez-vous chez le dentiste demain.** I have an appointment with the dentist tomorrow.

- **Pourquoi ? Tu … mal aux dents ?** Why? Do you have a toothache?

- **Non, je … mal. Une simple visite de contrôle.** No, I don't. Just a regular check-up.

…

3. - **Est-ce que tu … un animal domestique ?** Do you have a pet?

- **Oui, nous … un chien.** Yes, we have a dog.

…

4. - **Elle … de la chance avec son travail.** She is lucky with her job.

Oui, tu … raison. C'est bien payé et pas trop fatigant. Yes, you are right. It is well paid and not too tiring.

…

5. - **Est-ce que … un grenier dans la maison ?** Is there an attic in the house?

-**No, …. .** No, there isn't.

…

6. - **Quel age … ses enfants ?** How old are her children?

- **Je pense que le garçon … au moins 10 ans, et la fille est un peu plus jeune.** I think the boy is at least 10, and the girl is a bit younger.

…

7. -**… beaucoup d'espace pour les enfants dans ce parc.** There is a lot of space for children in this park.

- **Oui, ils … suffisamment de terrain de jeu.** Yes, they have a big enough playground.

DIALOGUE « Looking for a music shop »

Peter is walking one day in Paris looking for a music shop.

- Excusez-moi, **est-ce qu'il y a** un magasin de musique dans les environs ?

- Excuse me, is there a music shop nearby?

- Attendez, je réfléchis un instant...
Oui, **il y en a un** qui n'est pas loin.

- Let me think... Yes, there is one not far away from here.

- Comment je peux y aller ?

- How can I get there?

- D'abord allez tout droit, puis prenez la première à droite. Vous dépassez un grand supermarché et vous continuez jusqu'aux feux. Aux feux tournez à gauche sur boulevard Saint-Michel, le magasin de musique est à votre droite, en face du cinéma.

- Well, you go straight on, then take the first right. Go past a big supermarket and continue until you get to the traffic lights. At the traffic lights turn left onto boulevard Saint-Michel, and the music shop is on the right, opposite the cinema.

- Merci beaucoup !

- Thanks a lot!

- Je vous en prie ! Bonne journée !

- No problem. Have a nice day!

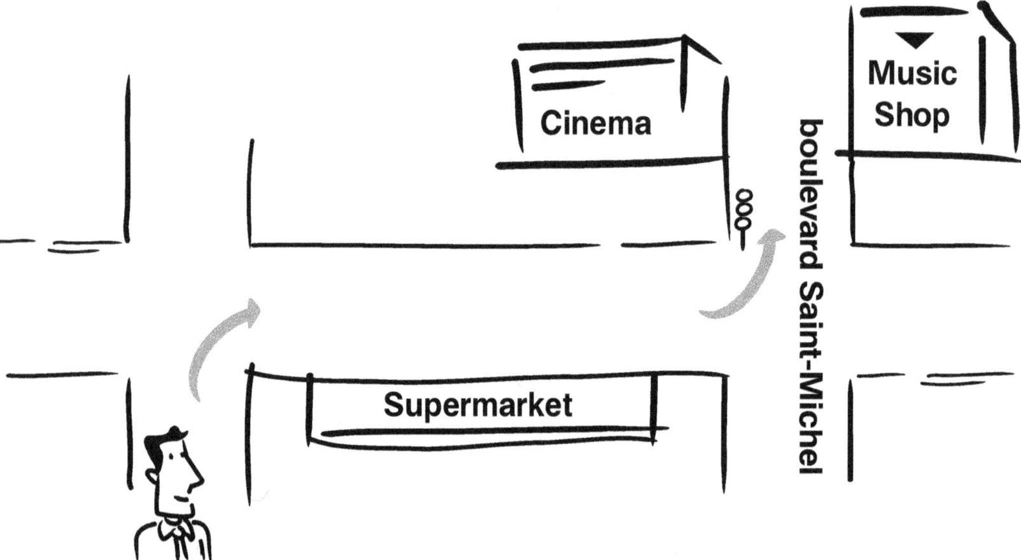

USEFUL VOCABULAIRY : giving directions

<u>Demander son chemin – Asking for directions</u>

Excusez-moi, comment je peux aller jusqu'à…? Excuse me, how can I get to…?

Pourriez-vous me dire comment aller jusqu'à…? Could you tell me how to get to ?

Excusez-moi, est-ce qu'il y a une pharmacie dans les environs ? Excuse me, is there a pharmacy nearby?

> **allez tout droit** – go straight ahead ; **puis** – then ; **prenez la première à gauche** – take the first left ; **prenez la deuxième à droite** – take the second right ; **passez à côté de...** – go past …; **c'est du côté gauche de la rue** – it's on the left side of the street; **c'est du côté droit** – it's on the right; **continuez jusqu'à**… – continue until you get to ... ; des **feux** – traffic lights ; **un passage piéton** – pedestrian crossing ; **aux feux tournez à droite** – at the traffic lights turn right ; **allez sur**...- go along ; **traversez la rue** – cross the street ; **au coin**- at the corner ; **à côté de** – next to ; **en face** – opposite **entre** – between

We are all equiped with *Gps, Google maps*, etc, but sometimes we cannot rely on technologies so it is useful to learn how to help someone find their way and understand when someone is giving you directions ☺

Always remember that the only way to improve your level of understanding is **to listen, to listen and to listen** – video and audio clips, films, TV and radio programmes, anything you find interesting.

UNIT 6

TEMPS – weather and time

The French have only one word for weather and time – **temps**.

A. <u>TEMPS</u> – weather

QUEL TEMPS IL FAIT ?
WHAT IS THE WEATHER LIKE?

Il fait beau. The weather is nice.

Il fait chaud. It is hot. (**une chaleur** – heat ; **une sécheresse** – drought)
Il fait froid. It is cold.
Il y a du soleil. It is sunny.. (**un lever du soleil** – sunrise ; **un coucher du soleil** –
sunset)
C'est nuageux. It is cloudy. (**des nuages** – clouds)
Il y a du vent. It is windy. (**un vent** – wind ; **un ouragan** – hurricane)
Il y a du brouillard. It is foggy.
Il pleut. It is raining. (**une pluie** – rain ; **un arc-en-ciel** – rainbow ; **un orage** –
storm ; **un éclair** – lightening ; **un tonnerre** – thunder ; **une inondation** – flood)
Il neige. It is snowing. (**une neige** – snow ; **un flocon** – snowflake
un bonhomme de neige – snowman ; **une grêle** – hail)

> **Est-ce qu'il fait froid** là-bas ? Is it hot there?
> **Est-ce qu'il neige** là-bas ? Is it snowing there?

Other words connected with the weather :

un ciel – sky ; **une étoile** – star ; **geler** – freeze ; **une température de l'air** – air
temperature ; **au-dessous de zéro / au-dessus de zéro** – below zero/above zero
la météo – weather forecast
selon la météo – according to the weather forecast
un ciel dégagé – clear sky ; **un ciel couvert** – overcast ; **des averses** – showers

Before talking about the time, let's see the numbers.

CARDINAL AND ORDINAL NUMBERS
HOW TO PRONOUNCE DATES, YEARS

nombre – number ; **chiffre** – figure/digit

The figures are, by definition, the symbols from 0 to 9 which help to form numbers.

597 est un nombre à trois chiffres. 597 is a three-digit number.

numérique – digital

Numbres Cardinaux et Ordinaux

1	un	premier, e
2	deux	deuxième/second, e
3	trois	troisième
4	quatre	quatrième
5	cinq	cinquième
6	six	sixième
7	sept	septième
8	huit	huitième
9	neuf	neuvième
10	dix	dixième
11	onze	onzième
12	douze	douzième
13	treize	treizième
14	quatorze	quatorzième
15	quinze	quinzième
16	seize	seizième
17	dix-sept	dix-septième
18	dix-huit	dix-huitième
19	dix-neuf	dix-neuvième
20	vingt	vingtième
30	trente	trentième
40	quarante	quarantième
50	cinquante	cinquantième
60	soixante	soixantième
70	soixante-dix	soixante-dixième
80	quatre-vingts	quatre-vingtième
90	quatre-vingt-dix	quatre-vingt-dixième
100	cent	centième

21 – vingt-et-un

32 – trente-deux

69 – soixante-neuf

83 – quatre-vingt-trois

Attention to 70+ and 90+ !

In difference to the other numbers (20, 30, 40, 50, 60, 80) where you only add un, deux, trois, etc., with 70 and 90 you have to use the numbers from 11 to 19.

73 - soixante-treize

77 - soixante-dix-sept

91 - quatre-vingt-onze

95 - quatre-vingt-quinze

200 deux-cents ; 300 trois-cents (cents with « s » !)

130 cent-trente

591 cinq-cent-quatre-vingt-onze (cent without « s » !)

1000 mille

2000 deux-mille (mille without « s » !)

3786 trois-mille-sept-cent-quatre-vingt-six

100 000 cent-mille

1000000 un million; 3000000 trois millions (millions with « s » !)

1000000000 un milliard

Saying phone numbers

The French usually pronounce phone numbers <u>by</u> **pairs**:

07-82 -95-46-79 – zero sept / quatre-vingt deux / quatre-vingt-quinze / quarante-six / soixante-dix-neuf

It can be quite difficult for a non-native speaker, especially because of the complicated 70+ and 90+.

Until you get more confident, you can say them the easier way – by separate digits. And to improve your capability to understand, you need **to listen** to original French as much as possible.

Les années – Years

Pronouncing years is easy, it is like pronouncing any number – you start with the thousands, then the hundreds, and so on.

1879 – mille-huit-cent-soixante-dix-neuf

1957 – mille-neuf-cent-cinquante-sept

1600 – mille-six-cents

1905 – mille-neuf-cent-cinq

2000 – deux-mille

2011 – deux-mille-onze

2020 – deux-mille-vingt

dans les années quatre vingt-dix – in the 90s

Les dates – dates

In difference with English, dates in French are said by <u>cardinal numbers</u> (le deux, le quatre, le dix, etc) with only one exception : 1er (le premier).

Attention !

When you say a date, you always start with the article « **le** »!

le 14 (quatorze) juillet – the fourteenth of July;

le 3 (trois) janvier – the third of January.

le 17 (dix-sept) mars – the seventeenth of March

But : le 1er (premier) janvier – the first of January

Je suis né le 21 avril. I was born on 21 April.

Décimales – Decimals

1/2 une moitié

1/3 un tiers

7.5 sept point cinq

B. TEMPS – time

QUELLE HEURE EST-IL ?
WHAT'S THE TIME?

Il est... – It is...

The main difference with English is that in French you always start with the hour and then you say the minutes.

10.30

Il est dix heures trente (formal) = dix heures et demie (informal)

11.15

Il est onze heures quinze (formal) = onze heures et quart (informal)

16.45

Il est seize heures quarante-cinq (formal) = dix-sept heures moins cinq (informal)

Instead of saying 5pm or 8pm, the French prefer to use the big numbers: 17 heures or 20 heures, or in a informal way they can say « 5 heures l'après-midi » or « 8 heures le soir »

Attention !

et demie – half past

et quart – quater past

With any other minutes in the right half of the clock there is no « et »

10.5 – il est dix heures cinq (not et cinq)

9.25 – il est neuf heures vingt- cinq

moins (in the left half of the clock)

moins le quart – a quarter to

moins dix – ten to

Il est...heures

Il est...heures **moins dix**............Il est...heures **dix**

Il est...heures **moins le quart**......Il est...heures **et quart**

Il est...heures **moins vingt**......Il est...heures **vingt**

Il est...heures **et demie**

Il est cinq heures / il est dix-sept heures

Il est cinq heures dix.

Il est cinq heures et quart

Il est cinq heures et demie

Il est six heures moins vingt

Il est six heures moins le quart

Il est six heures moins dix

Il est six heures moins cinq

<u>A quelle heure</u>... ? What time...?

<u>à</u> – at.

Le film commence <u>à</u> 20 heures. The film starts at 8pm.

midi – noon ; **minuit** – midnight

JOURS de la semaine ; mois ; saisons

<u>Jours de la semaine</u> -

Days of the week

lundi

mardi

mercredi

jeudi

vendredi

samed

dimanche

When the meaning is « next », there is no preposition:

On se voit **samedi**. I'll see you on Saturday.

If you put the article « le » with a day of the week, it means « every »

Je joue au tennis **le samedi**. I play tennis on Saturdays.

<u>**Mois**</u> – Months

With the preposition <u>**en**</u>:

en

        Janvier
        Février
        Mars
        Avril
        Mai
        Juin
        Juillet
        Aout
        Septembre
        Octobre
        Novembre
        Décembre

<u>**Saisons**</u> – Seasons

au printemps – in spring

en été – in summer

en automne – in autumn

en hiver – in winter

<u>**Années**</u> – Years

With the préposition <u>**en**</u>

en 2001

en 1893

dans les années 80 – in the 80s

au XXe siècle – in the 20th century

Without preposition:

la semaine prochaine / le mois prochain / l'année prochaine – next week/month/year

la semaine passée / l'année passée – last week/last year

cette semaine / ce mois / cette année – this week/month/year

chaque jour = tous les jours – every day

hier – yesterday

aujourd'hui – today

demain – tomorrow

UNIT 7
QUI, QU'EST-CE QUE, OÙ...

QUESTION WORDS

The question "words" are actually pronouns and adverbs but we call them words to simplify things.

<u>QUI</u> – WHO

With **qui** we ask about <u>people</u>.

Qui est le meilleur joueur de soccer aux Etats Unis ? Who is the best soccer player in the USA?

Qui sont les nouveaux dirigeants ? Who are the new managers?

<u>QUE / QU'EST-CE QUE</u> – WHAT

With **qu'est-ce que** we ask about <u>things</u>.
Qu'est-ce que c'est ? What is this?

<u>QUEL, QUELLE, QUELS, QUELLES</u> – WHICH

These question words agree with the noun in gender and number.

Quelle robe je dois choisir ? Which dress should I choose?
A quelle heure... ? What time..?
A quelle heure part ton train ? What time does your train leave?

Quel âge – How old
Quel âge a-t-il ? How old is he?

A quelle distance – how far
A quelle distance se trouve Chicago de New York ? How far is Chicago from New York?

<u>Lequel, laquelle, lesquels, lesquelles</u> – <u>which one</u>

Toutes tes robes sont belles. **Laquelle** est ta préférée ? All your dresses are beautiful. Which one is your favourite?

A qui – whose

Ce livre est **à qui** ? Whose is this book?

Où – where

Où es-tu ? Where are you?

Quand – when

Quand tu as commencé à apprendre le français ? When did you start learning French?

Pourquoi – why

Pourquoi tu veux apprendre le français ? Why do you want to learn French?

Comment – how

Comment vas-tu ? How are you?

Combien – How much / how many

It is used for both countable and uncountable nouns.
Combien ça coûte ? How much does it cost?
Combien de personnes ont participé au marathon ? How many people took part in the marathon?

Combien de temps / depuis quand – How long

Combien de temps vous avez vécu en Angleterre ? How long did you live in England?

Depuis quand tu habites en Angleterre ? How long have you lived in England?

Pour qui, avec qui, de quoi, d'où

The preposition is always placed before the question word:

D'où es-tu ? Where are you from?
Avec qui tu as parlé ? Who did you talk to?
A qui as-tu envoyé le mail ? Who did you send the mail to?
De quoi avez-vous parlé ? What did you talk about?

The choice of preposition depends on the verb. You will find some verbs with "their" prepositions in the Annex.

UNIT 8

ME, TE, LA, LUI, MOI...

PERSONAL PRONOUNS

The personal pronouns which can replace an object in the sentence are a bit complicated in French. Sometimes, one English form matches with three different forms in French. For example: **la, lui, elle** are all translated by « her » in English. Fortunately, there are strict rules with no exceptions.

subject pronouns		object pronouns			
	translation	direct object	translation	indirect object	translation
je	I	**me**	me	**me**	me
tu / vous	you	**te**	you	**te**	you
il	he / it	**le**	him / it	**lui**	him
elle	she / it	**la**	her / it	**lui**	her
nous	We	**nous**	us	**nous**	us
vous	You	**vous**	you	**vous**	you
ils/elles	they	**les**	them	**leur**	them

Contracted forms are used before a noun which begins with a vowel or h "muet":

me = m'   **te = t'**   **le = l'**   **la = l'**

l' can replace both masculine pronoun **le** and feminine pronoun **la**. The meaning would be clear only from the context.

<u>What is the difference between a direct and an indirect object?</u>

A direct object is directly linked to the verb, without a preposition. For example: I called Pierre, I watched the movie, etc.

J'ai pris le sac. I took the bag.

Je **l'ai** pris. I took it. (l' = le)

Harry aime Megan. Harry loves Megan.

Il **l'aime**. He loves her. (l' = la)
Je **t'aime**. I love you. (t' = te)

There is not always an exact match between the two languages – some French verbs followed by a direct object correspond to English verbs followed by preposition.

J'ai écouté la chanson. I listened to the song.
Je **l'ai** écoutée. I listened to it.

<u>Word order with direct object pronouns</u>

In difference with English, the direct object pronoun usually comes BEFORE the verb. In compound verb tenses, it is placed before the auxiliary verb "avoir".

Je ne **la** connais pas très bien. I don't know her very well.
Il **m'**a aidé. He helped me.

If there are two verbs in the sentence and the second verb is in infinitive, the pronoun is placed <u>before the infinitive</u>.
Je veux **les inviter** à la fête. I'd like to invite them to the party.
Je peux **vous aider**? May I help you? (formal)

<u>Attention!</u> In orders (imperatives) the pronoun is placed <u>at the end</u>, and **moi** is used instead of **me**, and **toi** - instead of **te**.

Aide-**moi**! Help me!
Prends **le**! Take it!

<u>Special use of **le**</u>

Le is sometimes used to refer back to an idea or information that has already been given. In these cases it is not translated in English.
Tu crois qu'ils vont augmenter les taxes ? Oui, je **le** pense vraiment.
You believe that they are going to raise taxes? Yes, I think so.

<u>Indirect object</u>

An indirect object is linked to the verb with a preposition. In English the preposition is usually "**to**". For example:
I gave a present **to** my girlfriend.
I talked **to** my colleagues about the project.

In French the preposition is usually "**à**":
J'ai donné un cadeau **à** ma petite amie.
J'ai parlé **à** mon collègue du projet.

The indirect object pronoun replaces an indirect object (a person or an animal).

Je **lui** ai donné un cadeau. I gave her a present.

Je **lui** ai parlé du projet. I talked to him about the project.

The pronoun comes BEFORE the verb. In compound verb tenses - before the auxiliary "avoir". If there are two verbs in the sentence - before the second verb in infinitive.

Je **leur** envoie des cadeaux parfois. I send them presents sometimes.

Je **lui** ai écrit une longue lettre. I wrote him (her) a long letter.

Je vais **lui** dire la vérité. I am going to tell him (her) the truth.

<u>Direct and indirect object pronouns in the same sentence</u>

Word order in a sentence with both direct and indirect pronouns is:

1. indirect object pronoun, 2. direct object pronoun, except for 3rd person singular and plural where it is vice versa:

Il **me le** donne. He is giving it to me.

Il **te le** donne. He is giving it to you.

Il **nous le** donne. He is giving it to us.

Il **vous le** donne. He is giving it to you. (you – plural)

BUT

Il **le lui** donne. He is giving it to him (her).

Il **le leur** donne. He is giving it to them.

Objects, preceded by another preposition (**avec** (with), **pour** (for), **sans** (without), **etc.**) can be replaced by a different type of pronouns:

moi	toi	lui	elle	nous	vous	eux, elles
me	you	him	her	us	you	them

Il habite **avec elle**. He lives with her.

Je ne peux pas vivre **sans toi**. I can't live without you.

As you can see, French pronouns are more difficult than the English ones. Which pronoun has to be used depends on the verb. We are going to study a lot of verbs further, illustrated with examples so you will gradually get used to the pronouns. And most importantly – to continue improving your French, you need **to read and to listen as much as possible**.

<u>Moi, toi, lui, elle…</u> – used for emphasizing

The pronouns **moi, toi, lui**… are used after a preposition but you can also put them at the very beginning of the sentence when you want to emphasize:

Moi, je n'aime pas l'opera ! I do not like opera!

Toi, tu as toujours froid. You are always cold.

ON, TU, ILS
GENERIC PERSONAL PRONOUNS

These pronouns are used when we speak in general, and are similar to the English « one, you, they »

On peut utiliser Internet sans comprendre les cookies. One can use the Internet without understanding cookies.

On ne sait jamais. You never know.

Tu ne peux pas toujours faire ce que tu veux. You can't always do what you want to. (in general)

Ils sont en train d'abattre les forêts. They are chopping down the rainforests.

Ils ont ouvert un nouveau cinema à côté. They have opened a new cinema nearby.

Y AND EN
SPECIFIC FRENCH PRONOUNS

These two pronouns which exist only in French can replace a noun or a clause in a sentence.

Y

1. Replaces a noun introduced by « **à** », « **en** », very often with the verb **aller**:

Tu vas <u>en Espagne</u> donc? So you are going to Spain?

Oui, **j'y vais**. (y = en Espagne)

Tu veux aller à la fête ? Do you want to go to the party?

Non, je ne veux pas **y aller**. (**y** = à la fête)

2. With the verbs **penser à** (think of), **croire à** (believe in), **s'intéresser à (**be interested in**), s'habituer à** (get used to)

Je pense à mon travail. I'm thinking of my job.

N'y pense pas ! Don't think about it!

y = à mon travail

N'y crois pas ! Don't believe in this!

y = in this

EN

1. Replaces an uncountable noun, introduced by « **du** », « **de la** », « **des** ».
Est-ce que tu veux du sucre pour ton café ? Would you like some sugar for the coffee ?

Oui, **j'en veux** un peu. Yes, I'd like a little bit.

en = du sucre

Est-ce qu'il reste du lait ? Is there any milk left?

Non, **il n'en reste plus**. No, there isn't any left.

en = du lait

Tu as des amis au Canada ? Do you have any friends in Canada?

Non, **je n'en ai pas**. No, I don't.

en = des amis

2.Replaces a noun or an expression following the verb « **parler de** » (talk about).

Vous avez parlé de la crise ? Did you talk about the crisis?

Oui, **on en a parlé**. Yes, we did.

en = de la crise

N'en parlons plus ! Let's not talk about this anymore!

en = about this

In theory EN is also used with verbs of movement and the preposition « de », like for example **venir de** (come back from) but this use is rare:

Je viens de la banque. **J'en** viens. I am coming back from the bank

As these two pronouns **Y** and **EN** are typical French, they are used in a completely natural way by native speakers, and at the same time, they are rather difficult for learners. If you master them, it means you have high level of proficiency in French ☺

<u>Some useful expressions with **Y** and **EN**</u>

Il s'y connait. He is competent in this matter.

Je n'y suis pour rien. It is not my fault.

Ça y est ! That's it! / It's over!

Allons-y ! Let's go!

Tu n'y es pas. You don't understand.

Je m'en vais. I am leaving.

Je m'en fiche. I don't care.

J'en ai assez. / J'en ai marre. (colloquial) I am fed up.

Je n'en peux plus. I can't handle it anymore.

Je lui en veux. I am angry with him.

Ne t'en fais pas ! Don't worry!

UNIT 9

MON, MA, TON, TA, SON, SA...

POSSESSIVE ADJECTIVES AND PRONOUNS

The possessive adjectives and pronouns in French agree with the noun in gender and number. There are also different forms depending on whether an object is owned by one person or by several people.

What is the difference between a possessive adjective and a possessive pronoun?

1. Possessive adjectives always accompany a noun:

ma sœur – my sister ; **leur** maison – their house ; **ses** parents – his parents

2. Possessive pronouns are independent and are used to avoid repetition of an already mentioned noun:

Leur voiture, c'est une Toyota, et **la nôtre** – une Ford. Their car is Toyota, and ours – Ford.

	Adjectives (accompany a noun)			
	one possession		several possessions	English translation
	masc.	fem.		
one possessor	**mon**	**ma**	**mes**	my
	ton	**ta**	**tes**	your
	son	**sa**	**ses**	his/her/its
several possessors	**notre**		**nos**	our
	votre		**vos**	your
	leur		**leurs**	their

Ma sœur s'appelle Jane. My sister's name is Jane.

Notre école est tout près. Our school is near here.

Leur fils est ingénieur. Their son is an engineer.

Nos amis s'intéressent à l'écologie. Our friends are interested in ecology.

Tes parents sont très sympa. Your parents are very nice.

Votre professeur vous fait travailler beaucoup. Your teacher makes you work hard

Pronouns (independant)					
	one possession		several posessions		English translation
	masc.	fem.	masc.	fem.	
one possessor	**le mien**	**la mienne**	**les miens**	**les miennes**	mine
	le tien	**la tienne**	**les tiens**	**les miennes**	yours
	le sien	**la sienne**	**les siens**	**les siennes**	his/hers/its
several possessors	**le nôtre**	**la nôtre**	**les nôtres**		ours
	le vôtre	**la vôtre**	**les vôtres**		yours
	le leur	**la leur**	**les leurs**		theirs

Ton sac est plus grand que **le mien**. Your bag is bigger than mine.

Mon fils a 5 ans, et **le sien** est encore bébé. My son is 5 years old, and hers is still a baby.

EXERCISES — Complete the gaps:

1. – Tu sais que Lili … un nouveau petit ami ? Do you know that Lili has a new boyfriend?

- C'est vrai ? Raconte-moi plus. Does she? Tell me a bit more.

- Euh, je…ai vus hier soir dans un café. Il est grand, blond, avec des yeux bleus. Well, I saw them last night in a cafe. He is tall and has blue eyes and blonde hair.

- Est-ce qu'il est étudiant comme … ? Is he a student like her?

- Oui, … vont à la même université. Yes, they go to the same university.

…

2. - … voisins ont une Lamborghini toute neuve ! Our neighbours have a brand-new Lamborghini!

- Waou! Est-ce que… est belle ? Wow! Is it nice?

- Elle est fantastique ! Je pense que … mari est un peu jaloux. It is fantastic! I think my husband is a bit jelous….

…

3. - … sœur est fâchée contre …. My sister is angry with me.

- Ah bon, et pourquoi ? Is she? Why?

- Je n'ai aucune idée. Elle fait la tête tout le temps. Je ne peux jamais… comprendre. I have no idea. She is always grumpy. I can never understand her.

…

4. – Nous … un nouveau chef au bureau. We have a new boss at work.

- Est-ce qu'il est sympa ? Is he cool?

- Oui, je … aime bien. Il … jeune et gentil. Yes, I like him. He is young and friendly.

…

5. – Elle fait des accessoires déco et … vend. She makes decorative accessories and sells them.

- Je sais, j'ai déjà acheté de très belles choses chez …. I know, I've bought some very nice things from her.

6. – Est-ce que tu as pris ... maillot de bain ? Did you take your swimming costume?

- Oh non, je ... oublié ! Oh no, I forgot it!

...

7. - ... soeur est tres sympa. Your sister is very nice.

Où est-ce que tu ...as vue? Where did you see her?

Je ne ... ai pas vue, j'ai parlé avec ... au téléphone. I have not seen her, I talked to her on the phone.

...

8. - ... frère et ..., nous avons beaucoup de chance. ... parents sont toujours disponibles pour ... My brother and I, we are lucky. Our parents are always there for us.

- C'est super! Les ... n'ont pas de temps pour .... . That's great! Mine do not have time for me.

...

9. - Est-ce que ce vélo est à ...? Is this bicycle yours?

- Non, ... est dans le garage. No, mine is in the garage.

CHAPTER 10
PRÉSENT

Translated in english by **Present simple** (I work), **Present continuous** (I am working), sometimes by **Present perfect** (I have worked) or **Present perfect continuous** (I have been working)

There are fewer verb tenses in French than in English. Their use is clearly defined so in this aspect it is much easier than English. Le **Présent** corresponds to <u>four</u> English tenses! What is still a bit complicated is the conjugation. The endings for each person singular and plural (I, you, he/she, we, they) vary but there are rules so it is not that difficult.

We use le **Présent** any time we talk about a present action, no matter if it is true in general or it is happening at the moment, or it has been happening for a while.

<u>HOW</u>
<u>DO WE FORM IT ?</u>

Affirmative

It is formed **from the infinitive** of the verb. We remove its ending and replace it with other endings for each person singular and plural.

There are <u>3 groups</u> of verbs, and some rules about each group:

I group

Verbs in the I group end in **-er**. A large number of verbs commonly used in every day speech are in this group, like for example:

parler (speak/talk) ; **aimer** (love) ; **regarder** (look) ; **écouter** (listen) ; **acheter** (buy); **appeler** (call) ; **jouer** (play) ; **manger** (eat) ; **commencer** (begin), etc.

They form **le Présent** with the following endings for each person singular and plural:

je	**-e**	nous	**-ons**
tu	**-es**	vous	**-ez**
il/elle	**-e**	ils/elles	**-ent**

Attention !

The endings **-e, -es, -e** (for singular) and **-ent** (for plural 3rd person) are **NOT pronounced**!

-ons is a nasal sound [oɳ] and **-ez** is [e] like in « n**e**st »

parler

je parl**e**	nous parl**ons**
tu parl**es**	vous parl**ez**
il/elle parl**e**	ils/elles parl**ent**

Je parle souvent au téléphone. I often talk on the phone.

Ils aiment se promener le soir. They love going for a walk in the evening.

Some specific cases:

Verb infinitives containing « e » without an accent, like **acheter**, **peser**.

The « e » in some of the conjugated forms (je, tu, il, elle, ils) gets an accent and **is** pronounced:

acheter

J'ach**è**te	nous achetons
Tu ach**è**tes	vous achetez
Il/elle ach**è**te	ils/elles ach**è**tent

appeler, jeter

The « e » in some of the forms (je, tu, il, elle, ils) is pronounced, because it is followed by a **doubled** consonant:

<u>appeler</u>

J'app**elle**	nous appelons
Tu app**elles**	vous appelez
Il/elle app**elle**	ils/elles app**ellent**

<u>II group</u>

Verbs in the II group end in **<u>-ir</u>**, like **choisir** (choose)

They form **le Présent** with the following endings for each person singular and plural:

-is	-issons
-is	-issez
-it	-issent

<u>choisir</u>

je chois**is**	nous chois**issons**
tu chois**is**	vous chois**issez**
il/elle chois**it**	Ils/elles chois**issent**

Similar : **agir** (act), **finir** (finish), **réussir** (succeed), **guérir** (recover), **fournir** (deliver), **remplir** (fill in), **unir** (unite).

<u>Attention to the exceptions!</u>

Some verbs whose infinitives end in **-ir** are irregular and are not conjugated with the typical endings of the II group. Examples: **courir** (run), **ouvrir** (open), **tenir** (hold). They belong to the following III group:

III group

This is the group of the **irregular verbs**!

They can end in:

-ir   **dormir** (sleep), **ouvrir** (open), **venir** (come)

-re   **répondre** (answer), **attendre** (wait), **vendre** (sell)

-**oir**   **voir** (see), **recevoir** (get), **vouloir** (want)

Most verbs in this group make the present tense with the following endings:

-s	-ons
-s	-ez
-t	-ent

However, several irregular verbs have to be learnt by heart. We have already studied **être** and **avoir**. Here are the other very important irregular verbs in alphabetic order. There are fewer irregular verbs than in English ☺

je **vais**	nous **allons**
tu **vas**	vous **allez**
il/elle **va**	ils/elles **vont**

boire – to drink

je **bois**	nous **buvons**
tu **bois**	vous **buvez**
il/elle **boit**	ils/elles **boivent**

connaître – to know

je **connais**	nous **connaissons**
tu **connais**	vous **connaissez**
il/elle **connaît**	ils/elles **connaissent**

Similar: **paraître** (appear/seem), **reconnaitre** (recognize/admit)

<u>**construire**</u> – to build

je **construis**	nous **construisons**
tu **construis**	vous **construisez**
il/elle **construit**	ils/elles **construisent**

Similar: **cuire** (cook/bake), **introduire** (introduce), **produire** (produce), **réduire** (decrease), **traduire** (translate), **détruire** (destroy)

<u>**croire**</u> – to believe

je **crois**	nous **croyons**
tu **crois**	vous **croyez**
il/elle **croit**	ils/elles **croient**

<u>**devoir**</u> – must

je **dois**	nous **devons**
tu **dois**	vous **devez**
il/elle **doit**	ils/elles **doivent**

<u>**dire**</u> – to say

je **dis**	nous **disons**
tu **dis**	vous **dites**
il/elle **dit**	ils/elles **disent**

Attention to « **vous dites** » ! The ending **-es** is NOT prononced ! This is a rare exception. Normally the ending for « vous » is -ez and is pronounced [e].

<u>**écrire**</u> – to read

j'**écris**	nous **écrivons**
tu **écris**	vous **écrivez**
il/elle **écrit**	ils/elles **écrivent**

Similar: **décrire** (describe), **prescrire** (prescribe)

faire – to do/make

je **fais**	nous **faisons**
tu **fais**	vous **faites**
il/elle **fait**	ils/elles **font**

Attention to « **vous faites** » ! « Vous faites » and « vous dites » are the two exceptions with an ending **-es** which is NOT pronounced!

Similar: **refaire** (do again), **satisfaire** (satisfy)

lire – to read

je **lis**	nous **lisons**
tu **lis**	vous **lisez**
il/elle **lit**	ils/elles **lisent**

mettre – to put

je **mets**	nous **mettons**
tu **mets**	vous **mettez**
il/elle **met**	ils/elles **mettent**

Similar: **admettre** (admit), **permettre** (allow), **omettre** (omit)

Some verbs in **-ir** are conjugated like the regular verbs from 1st group:

ouvrir – to open

j'**ouvre**	nous **ouvrons**
tu **ouvres**	vous **ouvrez**
il/elle **ouvre**	ils/elles **ouvrent**

Similar: **découvrir** (discover), **couvrir** (cover), **souffrir** (suffer), **offrir** (offer)

<u>**plaire**</u> – to be liked

je **plais**	nous **plaisons**
tu **plais**	vous **plaisez**
il/elle **plaît**	ils/elles **plaisent**

<u>**pouvoir**</u> – can

je **peux**	nous **pouvons**
tu **peux**	vous **pouvez**
il/elle **peut**	ils/elles **peuvent**

<u>**prendre**</u> – to take

je **prends**	nous **prenons**
tu **prends**	vous **prenez**
il/elle **prend**	ils/elles **prennent**

Similar: **apprendre** (learn), **comprendre** (understand), **entreprendre** (undertake)

<u>**recevoir**</u> – to receive

je **reçois**	nous **recevons**
tu **reçois**	vous **recevez**
il/elle **reçoit**	ils/elles **reçoivent**

Attention : **ç (c cédille)** is used in some forms in order to keep pronouncing **c [s]**.

<u>**savoir**</u> – to know

je **sais**	nous **savons**
tu **sais**	vous **savez**
il/elle **sait**	ils/elles **savent**

<u>**sortir**</u> – to go out

je **sors**	nous **sortons**
tu **sors**	vous **sortez**
il/elle **sort**	ils/elles **sortent**

Similar: **dormir** (sleep), **partir** (leave), **servir** (serve), **sentir** (smell), **mentir** (lie), **courir** (run)

<u>**vendre**</u> – to sell

je **vends**	nous **vendons**
tu **vends**	vous **vendez**
il/elle **vend**	ils/elles **vendent**

Similar: **entendre** (hear), **attendre** (wait), **rendre** (return/make)

<u>**venir**</u> – to come

je **viens**	nous **venons**
tu **viens**	vous **venez**
il/elle **vient**	ils/elles **viennent**

Similar: **tenir** (hold), **soutenir** (support), **maintenir** (maintain), **obtenir** (obtain), **devenir** (become), **revenir** (come back), **se souvenir** (remember)

<u>**vivre**</u> – to live

je **vis**	nous **vivons**
tu **vis**	vous **vivez**
il/elle/on **vit**	ils/elles **vivent**

<u>**voir**</u> – to see

je **vois**	nous **voyons**
tu **vois**	vous **voyez**
il/elle **voit**	ils/elles **voient**

Similar: **revoir** (revise), **prévoir** (foresee, expect)

vouloir – to want

je **veux**	nous **voulons**
tu **veux**	vous **voulez**
il/elle **veut**	ils/elles **veulent**

The conjugation of these verbs has to be learnt perfectly as they are some of the most commonly used verbs in French. The easiest (and the most enjoyable) way to learn them is by **reading and listening as much as possible**!

Attention!

The use of « **on** » (followed by the same form as il/elle) is very common in colloquial French! It almost always replaces « nous » in everyday speech. It is also often used when we talk in general.

On dîne à quelle heure ? What time are we going to have dinner?

On refuse parfois d'accepter la réalité. Sometimes one refuses to accept reality.

VERBES PRONOMINAUX
PRONOMINAL (REFLEXIVE) VERBS

Pronominal verbs need a reflexive pronoun (myself, yourself, himself…). In French there are much more pronominal verbs than in English.

French reflexive pronouns are:

je	**me**
tu	**te**
il/elle	**se**
nous	**nous**
vous	**vous**
ils/elles	**se**

Example: <u>**se lever**</u> – to get up

je **me** lève	nous **nous** levons
tu **te** lèves	vous **vous** levez
il/elle **se** lève	ils/elles **se** lèvent

A lot of commonly used verbs are pronominal in French, but are not pronominal in English. The reflexive pronoun indicates that the subject is performing the action on himself/herself rather than on someone else.

se réveiller	to wake up
s'habiller	to get dressed
se laver	to wash
se sentir	to feel
se plaindre	to complain
se fâcher	to get angry
se taire	to be quiet
s'inquiéter	to worry
s'inscrire	to register
se rappeler	to remember
se marier	to get married
s'endormir	to fall asleep
se coucher	to go to bed

Je me réveille d'habitude à 7 heures. I usually wake up at 7am.

Ils se couchent tôt. They go to bed early.

When we talk about parts of the body, we do NOT use possessive adjectives as we do in English:

Je me lave les mains. I am washing my hands. (not ~~Je lave mes mains.~~)

Elle se brosse les cheveux. She is brushing her hair. (not ~~Elle brosse ses cheveux.~~)

Some pronominal verbs are <u>reciprocal</u>, meaning that two or more subjects act upon each other:

se connaître – to know each other

se regarder – to look at each other

s'aimer – to love each other

s'aider – to help each other

Nous nous connaissons très bien. We know each other very well.

Ils se regardent. They are looking at each other.

Ils s'aident beaucoup. They help each other a lot.

<u>Idiomatic</u> pronominal verbs

These verbs use the reflexive pronouns to create a different meaning (although sometimes close). Here are some examples:

s'en aller	to go away	aller	to go
s'amuser	to have fun	amuser	to amuse
s'appeler	to be named	appeler	to call
s'entendre	to get along	entendre	to hear
se mettre à	to begin to	mettre	to put

Pronominal verbs obey to the same rules of conjugation as all other verbs. Those which end in **-er**, are conjugated like all verbs in I group, and so on.

(-) <u>Forme negative</u>

ne…pas

Any French verb, no matter if it is regular or irregular, and no matter of the verb tense, makes its negative form the same way: with **ne….pas**. It is easier than in English as there are no « don't/doesn't/didn't ».

If the verb starts with a vowel, « **ne** » becomes « **n'** ».

je **n**'aime **pas**, tu **n**'aimes **pas…**vous **n**'aimez **pas…**

je **ne** veux **pas**, il **ne** veut **pas**, ils **ne** veulent **pas**

je **ne** comprends **pas**, elle **ne** comprend **pas**, nous **ne** comprenons **pas…**

If there is a negative word in the sentence, for example **jamais** (never), it replaces « pas », because you cannot have a double negation.

Je **ne** fume **jamais**. I never smoke.

(?) <u>Question form</u>

A question form is always made in one of the three ways that we have already seen in Unit 4 ETRE: **est-ce que, intonation** or **inversion**. « Est-ce que » is probably the most common, but the intonation is also often used, especially in everyday speech.

The inversion is rare but one classic question is an example of inversion:

Parlez-vous français ? Do you speak French?

Most often it is **est-ce que** at the beginning of the sentence or a rising intonation:

Est-ce que tu aimes le jazz ? Do you like jazz?

or

Tu aimes le jazz ?

Est-ce que tu comprends ? Do you understand ?

or

Tu comprends?

Est-ce qu'elle habite à New York ? Does she live in New York ?

If there is a <u>question word</u>, it comes before **est-ce que:**

Où est-ce qu'elle habite **?** Where does she live ?

Quand est-ce qu'ils arrivent ? When do they arrive ?

Another option is: interrogative intonation and the question word at the end.

Elle habite où ?

Ils arrivent quand ?

(- ?) <u>Negative question</u>

est-ce que and **ne...pas**

Est-ce que tu n'aimes pas le chocolat ? Don't you like chocolate ?

Tu ne veux pas venir avec moi ?! Don't you want to come with me ?!

Possible answers:

Non, je ne veux pas ! No, I don't!

Si, je veux venir avec toi ! Yes, I do want to come with you!

Attention !

« **Si** », not « ~~oui~~ », can be an answer to a negative question!

<u>Question tags</u>

..., n'est-ce pas ?

The French question tag is universal: for any verbs and any verbs tenses.

Tu aimes la France, **n'est-ce pas** ? You like France, don't you?

Il travaille toujours avec toi, **n'est-ce pas** ? He still works with you, doesn't he?

Negative form, question form, question tags, all these elements are easier in French than in English as they are always the same for present, past, future tenses, and for any person singular or plural.

Impératif

The imperative form depends on what type the verb is.

<u>Verbs I group</u>

<u>Regarder</u>

Regarde !
Regardez ! Look!
Regardons ! Let's look!

<u>Continuer</u>

Continue !
Continuez ! Keep going!
Continuons ! Let's continue!

<u>Verbs II group</u>

<u>Choisir</u>

Choisis !
Choisissez ! Choose!
Choisissons ! Let's choose!

<u>Verbs III group</u>

<u>Dire</u>

Dis !
Dites ! Say!
Disons ! Let's say!

<u>Prendre</u>

Prends !

Prenez ! Take!

Prenons ! Let's take!

<u>Pronominal verbs</u>

The imperative of pronominal verbs is similar but you should always add **toi, vous, nous**:

Lave-toi les mains !

Lavez-vous les mains ! Wash your hands!

Lavons-nous les mains ! Let's wash our hands!

Tais-toi !

Taisez-vous ! Be quiet!

Taisons-nous ! Let's be quiet!

<u>Negative form:</u>

In the negative form we keep the reflexive pronouns **te, vous, nous**:

Ne t'inquiète pas ! Don't worry!

Ne vous inquiétez pas !

Attention to the exceptions!

<u>Etre</u>

Sois patient !

Soyez patients ! Be patient!

Soyons patients ! Let's be patient!

Avoir

Aie ... !

       Have... !

Ayez ... !

Ayons ... ! Let's have... !

Aller

Va !

       Go!

Allez !

Allons ! Let's go!

Savoir

Sache que... !

       Know that... !

Sachez que... !

Negative form

The negative form is made with **ne...pas** for all verbs.

N'arrête pas ! Don't stop!

Ne parlez pas ! Don't speak!

Ne te fais pas de soucis ! Don't worry!

WHEN
DO WE USE **LE PRÉSENT** ?

1. Things in general, habits, skills, repeated actions.

Equivalent to *Present Simple* in English.

La lune tourne autour de la terre. The Moon goes round the Earth.

Je joue au tennis tous les dimanches. I play tennis every Sunday.

Ce magasin ouvre à 10 heures.This shop opens at 10 am.

Il parle trois langues. He speaks three languages.

Il se lève d'habitude à 7 heures.
He ususally gets up at 7am.

Il commence le travail à 9 heures.
He starts work at 9am.

Il promène le chien tous les soirs.
He walks the dog every evening.

2. Something which **is hapenning at the time of speaking.**

Equivalent to *Present Continuous*.

> **Je lis** un livre français. I am reading a French book.
> **Il répare** le vélo. He is repairing the bicycle.

There is, in fact, one structure which has exactly the same function as *Present Continuous* but it is optional. You can still say everything «au Présent». This structure is:

> **être en train de + infinitif** = Present Continuous

> **Je suis en train d'**écrire un mail. I am writing an email.
> **Ils sont en train de** regarder la télé. They are watching TV.

You would usually use this structure, if you want to put a special emphasis on what you are doing at the moment.

Elle est en train de faire la cuisine. Il regarde la télé.
She is cooking. He is watching TV.

Il est en train de nettoyer la maison.
He is cleaning the house.

The common question « What are you doing ? » is usually « au Présent » :

Qu'est-ce que tu fais ?

You can ask « Qu'est-ce que **tu es en train de faire** ? » in the case you are curious about what the other is doing or if you do not approve of it.

3. Something which **started in the past and is still continuing** in the present.

Equivalent to *Present Perfect or Present Perfect Continuous* in their use with since/ for.

Je les connais depuis 5 ans. I have known them for 5 years.

Ils habitent à New Jersey depuis 2011. They have lived in New Jersey since 2011.

Je joue au football depuis 10 ans. I have been playing football for 10 years.

4. **Future** – personal plans and arrangements, schedules and timetables.

Je pars à Boston demain matin. I am going to Boston tomorrow morning.

A quelle heure commence le match ? What time does the football match start?

Qu'est-ce que tu fais ce soir ? What are you doing tonight ?

Le participe présent and **le gérondif**

Le participe présent (present participle) and **le gérondif** (gerund) are similar to the English -**ing** form, but they do not take part in any verb tense and their use is much more limited than the -**ing** form.

Le participe présent = the stem of the 1st person plural (nous) + **-ant**

faire – nous **fais**-ons → **faisant** (doing)

Irregular verbs: être → **étant** (being); avoir → **ayant** (having); savoir → **sachant** (knowing)

Le gérondif = en + participe présent

en parlant (speaking); **en jouant** (playing); **en regardant** (looking)

En parlant de voitures, est-ce que tu es content de ta nouvelle Toyota?

Speaking of cars, are you happy with your new Toyota?

EXERCISES — Conjugate the verbs:

1. - ... tu ... (aller) toujours à tes cours de callanétics ? Do you still go to your callanetics class ?

- Oh, oui, ça m'aide à être en forme. Oh yes, I do. It helps me stay in good shape.

...

2. - Il ...(habiter) aux Etats Unis, ... ? He lives in the USA, doesn't he? (conversation about an ex-classmate)

- Oui, il ....(habiter) à Albuquerque, Nouveau Mexique. Yes, he lives in Albuquerque, New Mexico.

- ....il...(faire) là-bas ? What does he do there?

- Il ....(travailler) dans un centre de recherche scientifique. He works for a scientific research centre.

- .....il... (revenir) souvent en France ? Does he often come back to France?

- Pas très souvent – une fois par an ou tous les deux ans. Not very often – once a year or once every two years.

...

3. – Tu ...(faire) du sport ? Do you do any sport?

- Pas activement, mais on ... du ski tous les hivers avec les enfants. Well, not actively, but we go skiing every winter with the children.

- Où ...vous ... (aller) d'habitude ? Where do you usually go?

- A Vail. To Vail.

...

4. - ....elle ...(habiter) à San Francisco ? Does she live in San Francisco?

- Oui, mais elle ....(ne pas être née) là-bas. Yes, she does, but she was not born there.

- Où..... (être née) ? Where was she born?

- A la Nouvelle-Orléans. In New Orleans.

...

5. - Depuis quand vous ...(se connaitre) ? How long have you known each other?

- Depuis plus de 10 ans. For more than 10 years.

...

6. – Je ... (faire) une fête ce samedi. Tu veux venir ? I am having a party on Saturday. Would you like to come?

- Volontiers. Qui d'autre ...(venir) ? Sure. Who else is coming?

...

7. Tu … (savoir) qu'il y a un super film sur Canal+ en ce moment ? You know that there is a great film on Canal+ at the moment? (on the phone)

- Oui, je …. (savoir). Yes, I am watching it.

…

8. - Depuis quand tu … (aller) à tes cours de salsa ? How long have you been going to your salsa class?

- Depuis quelques mois. For a few months.

…

9. - Pourquoi tu es fâché ? Why are you grumpy?

- Je … (essayer) depuis une heure de comprendre comment télécharger une vidéo de Facebook, et je n'y arrive pas. I've been trying for one hour to figure out how to download a video from Facebook, and I can't.

- Ne t'inquiète pas ! Je vais te montrer. Take it easy! I'll show you.

…

10. - Est-ce que tu … (regarder) « The Voice » ? Do you watch The Voice?

- Oui, je … (regarder), et je… (aimer) beaucoup. Yes, I do, and I love it.

…

11. - Tu … (faire) quoi ? What are you doing ?

- Je … (preparer) pour mon entretien d'embauche. I am preparing for my job interview

…

12. - Je …(ne pas acheter) plus de journaux. I do not buy newspapers anymore.

- Mais tu … (lire) les actualités sur Internet, je suppose. But you read the news on the Internet, I guess.

- Oui, et je… (écouter) la radio le matin, avant d'aller au travail. Yes, and I listen to the radio in the morning before going to work.

….

13. – Je … (chercher) une petite table pour ma chambre. Je … (préférer) l'acheter sur Internet. I am looking for a little table for my room. I prefer to buy it online.

- Pourquoi tu … (ne pas vérifier) sur le site de Ikea ? Ils ont des choses sympa. Why don't you check the Ikea website? They have some nice things.

…

14. - …vous … (fumer) ? Do you smoke?

- Oui, je fume au moins un paquet par jour. Yes, I do. I smoke at least one pack a day.

A joke

Un homme âgé de 60 ans va faire son examen médical régulier, et après l'examen demande au docteur :

- Docteur, est-ce que vous pensez que je vais vivre encore 40 ans et atteindre 100 ?

- Ça dépend, répond le docteur. Vous fumez ?

- Non.

- Vous buvez ?

- Non.

- Vous faites souvent la fête?

- Plus maintenant.

- Eh bien alors, pourquoi, voulez-vous vivre jusqu'à 100 ans ?!

A 60-year-old man is getting his annual physical, and as they've just finished up he asks his doctor a frank question.

- Doc, do you think I'll live another 40 years so I can reach 100?
he asks.

- That depends, says the doctor. Do you smoke?

- No.

- Do you drink?

- No.

- Do you often go to parties?

- Not anymore.

- Well, then, says the doctor. Why do you want to live for another 40 years?!

DIALOGUE « Talking about football, tennis, work »

Au bistrot.

Peter and Olivier are going to watch a football match.

Peter : Salut, Olivier, comment ça va ?

Peter: Hi, Olivier, how are you?

Olivier : Très bien, merci, et toi ?

Olivier: Very well, thanks, and you?

Peter : Pas mal. J'ai eu une journée chargée au travail, et maintenant **j'ai envie de** me détendre. A quelle heure **commence** le match ?

Peter: Not too bad. I had a busy day at work and now I just want to relax. What time does the match start?

Olivier : A 20.30. Avant le match il y a d'habitude des journalistes et des experts qui **discutent**, font des commentaires sur la stratégie, les joueurs, les chances de chaque équipe de gagner.

Olivier: At 8.30pm. Journalists and sport experts usually have a talk before the game. They make comments on the strategy, the players, the chances of each team to win.

Peter : En fait, **je ne connais pas** le football européen très bien. Nous avons une équipe de « soccer », comme **on l'appelle** chez nous, mais **on regarde** notre football américain beaucoup plus souvent.

Peter: I do not know European football very well. We have a soccer team, of course, as it is called in my country but we watch our American football much more often.

Olivier : En France le football américain est presque inconnu. En revanche, **je connais** bien votre tennis. **J'admire** les joueurs légendaires du passé comme Pete Sampras et André Agassi et **je vois** que maintenant vous avez une nouvelle génération de joueurs très doués.

Olivier : In France American football is almost unknown. But I know your tennis well and I admire legendary players like Pete Sampras and Andre Agassi. I see that now you have a new generation of very talented players.

Peter : Moi aussi, **j'aime** le tennis, et j'aime jouer, pas seulement regarder.

Peter : Me too, I like tennis, and like playing, not just watching.

Olivier : C'est vrai? Le tennis, c'est ma passion ! **Je joue** tous les dimanches matin. Tu es le bienvenu de rejoindre notre club.

Olivier: Do you? Tennis is my passion! I play every Sunday morning. You are welcome to join our club.

Peter : Oh, merci, c'est très gentil! Mais **tu vas** le regretter probablement quand **je commence** à te battre !

Peter: Oh, thanks, that's very kind of you! But you will probably regret it when I start beating you!

Olivier : Haha, impossible ! J'ai beaucoup d'expérience, et puis **je fais** des efforts pour être en forme – **je cours** tous les matins.

Olivier: Haha, no way! I have a lot of experience plus I try hard to keep fit – I go jogging every morning.

Peter : Moi aussi. Bon, pas tous les jours, mais au moins trois fois par semaine. **Je me lève** à 6.30, je cours dans le parc, et

Peter: So do I. Well, not every day, but at least three times a week. I get up at 6.30am, go jogging in the park and then après **il me reste** suffisamment de temps pour me préparer à aller au travail.

I have enough time left to get ready for work.

Olivier : **Tu commences** le travail à quelle heure ?

Olivier: What time do you start work?

Peter : A 9 heures. Normalement **je dois** travailler jusqu'à 18 heures, mais **je reste** souvent jusqu'à 19 heures ou même plus tard.

Peter: At 9am. I'm supposed to work until 6pm but I often stay until 7pm or even later.

Olivier :
Moi aussi, mais **je peux** commencer plus tard le matin. J'ai en plus un jour de la semaine où je peux travailler de chez moi. D'habitude **je choisis** vendredi. Et le soir je viens ici, bien sûr.

Olivier:
Me too, but I can start late in the morning. I also have one day of the week when I can work from home. I usually choose Friday. And in the evening I am always here, of course.

USEFUL VOCABULARY : everyday life, free time, sport

Every day routine – Activités quotidiennes

se réveiller – to wake up ; **se lever** – to get up

prendre une douche – to have a shower

prendre son petit déjeuner – to have breakfast

aller au travail – to go to work ; **faire une pause** – to have a break

déjeuner – to have lunch ; **finir le travail** – to finish work

faire des courses – to do the shopping ; **rentrer à la maison** – to go home

dîner – to have dinner ; **aller au lit** – to go to bed

se coucher tôt – to have an early night ; **s'endormir** – to fall asleep

dormir – to sleep ; **rêver** – to dream

un emploi du temps – schedule

du temps libre – free time

Que fais-tu de ton temps libre ? What do you do in your free time?

At home – à la maison

écouter de la musique – to listen to music ; **écouter la radio** – to listen to <u>the</u> radio

regarder la télé – to watch TV ; **surfer sur Internet** – to surf the net

parler au téléphone – to chat on the phone

lire un livre / **un journal** / **un magazine** – to read a book / a newpaper / a magazine

faire des mots-croisés – to do crosswords

recevoir des invités – to invite friends

faire la cuisine – to cook ; **dîner avec des amis** – to have dinner with friends

commander un repas à emporter – to order a take-away

Go out – Sortir

aller au restaurant / **au bistrot**/ **dans un bar** – to go to a restaurant/ to the pub / to a nightclub

sortir dîner – to go out for dinner ; **sortir boire un verre** – to go out for a drink

aller à un match de football – to go to a football match

aller au cinéma / **au théâtre** / **au concert** – to go to the cinema/ to the theatre/ to a concert

se promener – to go for a walk ; **faire les magasins** – to go shopping

Est-ce que tu aimes…? Do you like…?

Tu aimes danser ? Do you like dancing?

Tu aimes jouer sur l'ordinateur ? Do you like playing computer games?

J'aime la randonnée. Et toi ? I like hiking. What about you?

Tu joues au tennis ? Do you play tennis?

Tu aimes le football ? Do you like football?

Est-ce que tu aimes lire ? Do you like reading?

Tu aimes quel type de musique ? What kind of music do you like?

Tu aimes quel genre de films ? What kind of movies do you like?

jouer – play

« Jouer » in French is like « play » in English – it is used for both sport and music.

jouer au tennis – to play tennis

jouer du piano – to play the piano

Attention to the preposition!

Jouer **au** – refers to sport

Jouer **du / de la** – refers to music

Sport

gagner – to win ; **un vainqueur** – winner ; **battre** – to defeat ; **perdre** – to lose
faire match nul – to draw

une compétition – competition ; **un tournoi** – tournament ; **un tournoi à la ronde**
– round-robin ; **une course** – race ; **un évènement sportif** – sport event

Tu fais du sport ? Do you play any sports?

Quel sport tu pratiques ? What sport do you do?

Quel est ton sport préféré ? What is your favourite sport?

l'athlétisme – athletics ; **la gymnastique** – gymnastics ; **l'haltérophilie** – weight
lifting ; **la lutte** – wrestling ; **l'équitation** – horse riding ; **le cyclisme** – cycling
les arts martiaux – martial arts

Sports nautiques – Water sports

la natation – swimming ; **la plongée** – diving ; **l'aviron** – rowing ; **le ski nautique**
– water skiing ; **la planche à voile** – windsurfing

la pêche – fishing ; **la chasse** – hunting ; **le tir** – shooting sport

Sports d'hiver – Winter sports

faire du ski – to go skiing ; **faire du patinage (sur glace)** – to go ice skating
une patinoire – ice rink ; **hockey sur glace** – ice hockey

<u>Sports extrêmes – Extreme sports</u>

la plongée sous-marine – scuba diving ; **le saut à l'élastique** – bungee jumping
l'escalade – climbing ; **le parachutisme** – sky diving

<u>Ski</u>

une station de ski – ski resort ; **une remontée mécanique** – lift ; **une piste de ski**
– ski slope/ski run

<u>Tennis</u>

un arbitre de chaise – chair umpire ; **un arbitre de ligne** – line judge ; **jeu** – game
set – set ; **avantage** – advantage ; **égalité** – dues (40-40)

FAIRE, **ALLER** or **JOUER** <u>– three verbs used with sports</u>

<u>Faire</u>

faire de la natation – to go swimming ; **faire du ski** – to go skiing ; **faire du yoga**
– to do yoga

<u>Aller</u>

aller à la pêche – to go fishing ; **aller danser** – to go dancing

<u>Jouer</u>

jouer au football / au volleyball / au tennis / au squash

jouer au bridge / jouer aux échecs (to play chess)

DIALOGUE « Suggestion for an evening out »

Olivier is calling Peter on Wednesday evening :

Olivier : Salut, Peter, **comment vas-tu** ? **Qu'est-ce que tu fais** ce soir ?

Olivier: Hi, Peter, how are you? What are you doing tonight?

Peter : Salut, Olivier, je n'ai pas de projets. **Je travaille** encore, **je dois** préparer une présentation pour demain.

Peter: Hi, Olivier, no plans at all. I am still working. I have to prepare one presentation for tomorrow.

Olivier : Un bon groupe va jouer ce soir au club, et nous **on y va. Tu ne veux pas venir** avec nous ?

Peter : Bonne idée, mais malheureusement **je dois** me lever à 4.30 demain matin pour prendre l'avion. **Je vais** en voyage d'affaires à Barcelone. Et donc, **je pense** que je devrais me coucher tôt. C'est dommage !

Olivier : **Ne t'inquiète pas**, tu pourras les voir une autre fois. D'habitude, **ils jouent** le samedi – c'est une exception aujourd'hui. Bon voyage à Barcelone !

Peter : Merci. **Amusez-vous** bien ce soir !

Olivier: There is a good band playing in the pub tonight and we are going. Why don't you come with us?

Peter: Great idea, but unfortunately I have to get up at 4.30 tomorrow morning to catch a plane. I am going on a business trip to Barcelona. So I guess I'd better have an early night. Such a pity!

Olivier: Don't worry, you can see them another time. They usually play on Saturdays – it is an exception today. Have a nice trip to Barcelona!

Peter: Thanks! Have a good time tonight!

USEFUL VOCABULARY : telephone, letter, email, how to invite, to accept, to refuse

<u>Téléphone</u>

un portable un mobile – cell phone ; **appeler au téléphone** – to call / to phone ; **donner un coup de fil** – to ring / to give a ring ; **rappeler** – to call back ; **faire un numéro** – to dial

joindre quelqu'un – to get through

Je n'ai pas pu vous joindre. I could not get through.

Je vais vous rappeler plus tard. I'll call you back later.

un téléphone fixe – land line ; **un indicatif pays** – country code ; **un répondeur** – answering machine

Est-ce que je peux parler à ... ? Can I speak to ...?

Veuillez patienter, s'il vous plaît. Hold on please.

<u>Email</u>

écrire – to write; **envoyer un email** – to send an email ; **recevoir** – to receive **se connecter** – to sign in ; **se déconnecter** – to sign out ; **une boîte de réception** – inbox ; **un courrier indésirable** – spam ; **un brouillon** – draft

Here are some useful expressions you can use :

<u>Lettre informelle (email)- Informal Letter</u>

<u>At the beginning</u>

Chère Sara – Dear Sara

Merci de ta lettre. Très content(e) d'avoir de tes nouvelles. Thanks for your letter. It was lovely to hear from you.

Comment vas-tu ? Comment ça va ? How are you? / How are things?

J'espère que tu vas bien. Hope you are well.

Je me réjouis de savoir que… Quelle bonne nouvelle… I'm so pleased to hear that... What wonderful news...

Je regrette d'apprendre que... I'm sorry to hear that...

Je t'écris pour te demander… La raison pour laquelle je t'écris... I'm writing to ask you... The reason I'm writing...

<u>At the end</u>

C'est tout pour le moment. That's all for now.

Réponds-moi vite. Write back soon.

J'espère que tu vas m'écrire bientôt. Hope to hear from you soon.

Bonne chance! Je te souhaite le meilleur ! Best wishes !

Ciao ! Cheers!

Fais une bise à… de ma part. Give my love to...

Passe le Bonjour à… de ma part. Say hello to...

Bisous / Gros bisous – Love / Lots of love (literally « kisses »)

<u>Lettre formelle /email – Formal Letter</u>

<u>Greetings</u>

A qui de droit – To whom it may concern

Monsieur, Madame – Dear Sir or Madam

Cher M. / Mme Blake – Dear Mr./Mrs Blake

Je vous écris au sujet de… I am writing with regard to

Replying

Merci pour votre intérêt... Thank you for your interest...

Nous vous remercions d'avoir contacté notre compagnie... Thank you for contacting our company...

Je vous remercie pour votre email au sujet de... Thank you for your email regarding...

A la suite de notre conversation au téléphone de ce matin... With reference to our phone conversation this morning...

Je vous écris en réponse à votre demande de renseignements sur... I am writing to respond to your inquiry about...

Vous allez trouver en pièce jointe... You will find attached...

Asking

Je vous serais bien reconnaissant si vous... I would be most grateful if you would...

J'apprécierai si vous pourriez... I would appreciate if you could...

Je me demande si vous pourriez... I was wondering if you could...

Est-ce que vous pourriez m'envoyer... Could you please send me...

S'excuser

Veuillez accepter nos sincères excuses pour ce retard. Please accept our sincere apologies for this delay.

Veuillez nous excuser pour tout inconvénient que cela a pu vous causer. We apologise for any inconvenience caused.

Complaining

Je voudrais me plaindre de... I would like to complain about...

Je vous écris pour exprimer mon mécontentement à l'égard de... I am writing to express my dissatisfaction with...

J'étais déçu(e) de trouver que... I was disappointed to find that...

At the end

Nous espérons que vous en êtes satisfait(e). We hope that you find this satisfactory.

N'hésitez pas de me contacter pour toute question supplémentaire / tout complément d'information. Please feel free to contact me, if you have any further questions.

Si vous avez besoin de plus d'informations, n'hésitez pas à nous contacter. If you require any further information, please do not hesitate to contact us.

J'attends votre réponse avec impatience. I am looking forward to hearing from you.

Veuillez agréer, Monsieur / Madame, l'expression de mes salutations distinguées. Yours faithfully

Veuillez agréer, Mr/Mme Blake, l'expression de mes salutations distinguées. Yours sincerely

Work email

Greetings

Bonjour

Informing

J'écris pour t' (vous) informer que... I'm writing to tell you about...

Un message pour te dire que... Just a note to say...

Juste pour te mettre au courant de... Just to update you on...

Asking

Je t'écris pour te demander... I'm emailing to ask you...

Est-ce que tu peux jeter un coup d'œil à... Could you look into...

Pourrais-tu vérifier... pour moi, s'il te plaît ? Would you mind checking... out for me?

J'aimerais bien avoir ton avis sur ce sujet. I'd love to hear your advice on this matter.

Est-ce que tu peux me contacter après avoir étudié ça ? Can you get back to me once you have examined this?

Tu peux m'écrire juste un mot pour que je sache que tu as reçu ça ? Can you drop me a quick word so I know you have received this?

Je me demandais si tu avais reçu mon mail... Just wondering if you got my email ...

Confirming

Je voudrais confirmer que... I'd like to confirm that...

Je vous écris pour confirmer que... I'm writing to confirm that...

<u>Changing plans</u>

Désolé, mais je ne pourrai pas venir mardi comme prévu. Est-ce qu'on peut reporter à mercredi ?

I'm sorry but I can't make it on Tuesday as expected. How about Wednesday instead?

<u>At the end</u>

J'espère que ça aide, mais rappelle-moi si tu continues à avoir des difficultés.

I hope this helps, but email me again if you are still having some difficulties.

Contactez-moi si vous avez des questions. Just let me know if you have any questions.

Ecris-moi ou appelle-moi, si tu as besoin de plus d'informations.

Drop me a line or give me a ring, if you need any more information.

On reste en contact. Keep in touch.

Tiens-moi au courant. Keep me posted.

Merci d'avance. Thanks in advance.

J'attends ta réponse. I look forward to hearing from you.

Cordialement – Best regards

Bien cordialement – Kind regards

Bien à vous, bien à toi – Regards

How to invite, to suggest

<u>Invitation / suggestion</u>

Est-ce que tu veux… ? Est-ce que vous voudriez… ? Would you like to + infinitive?

Tu veux venir au cinéma avec nous ? Would you like to come with us to the cinema?

Ça te dit de… ? Do you fancy + ing?

Ça te dit d'aller se promener ? Do you fancy going for a walk?

Et si on… ? How about + ing?

Si on allait au restaurant ce soir ? How about going to a restaurant tonight?

Allez… Let's…; **Allez, on sort** ! Let's go out!

Pourquoi ne pas + infinitif?

Pourquoi ne pas inviter ton frère ce soir ? Why don't we invite your brother tonight?

Accept – Accepter

Ça sera super. That would be great.

Bonne idée ! Good idea!

Super ! Great idea!

J'aimerais bien. I'd love to. ; **avec plaisir, volontiers** – with pleasure

Bien sûr – of course ; **naturellement** – sure

C'est bon, Je ne suis pas contre. I don't mind.

Refuse politely – Refuser poliment

Je suis vraiment désolé(e), mais je ne peux pas. I'm really sorry, but I can't.

Je crains de ne pas pouvoir, je dois… (formal) I'm afraid I can't, I have to…

Je voudrais bien, mais… I'd love to, but I…

Si on allait au cinéma au lieu d'aller au bistrot ? How about going to the cinema instead of going to the pub?

Agree – Être d'accord

Je suis d'accord avec toi (vous). I agree with you.

Oui, c'est vrai. Yes, that's right.

Bien sûr. Of course.

Exactement – Exactly ; **certainement** – certainly ; **définitivement** – definitely

Sans doute. No doubt.

Tu as raison (Vous avez raison). You are right.

Je vois. (je comprends). I see (= I understand).

Disagree / not agree – Ne pas être d'accord

Je ne suis pas d'accord avec toi (avec vous). I don't agree with you.

Non, jamais ! (informal) No, no way !

Tu n'as pas raison. (vous n'avez pas raison). You are not right / you are wrong.

Je ne pense pas que vous ayez raison. I don't think you are right.

Je ne pense pas. I don't think so.

C'est impossible. It's impossible.

CHAPITRE 11

OFFERING AND ASKING

WOULD YOU LIKE... ? CAN I HAVE... ?

There are a few questions for offering and asking politely, which are often used in everyday life:

Est-ce que tu veux... ?

Voulez-vous... ?   Would you like...?

Voudriez-vous... ?

Puis-je avoir...?
                                        Can I have....?
Est-ce que je peux avoir... ?

Est-ce que tu peux / vous pouvez... ?   Can you ...?

Pourriez-vous... ? (formal)   Could you... ?

DIALOGUE

« DANS UNE BOUTIQUE DE VÊTEMENTS »

Peter : Excusez-moi, **je peux essayer** la veste marron qui est dans la vitrine ?

Peter: Excuse me, can I try on the brown jacket in the window?

La vendeuse : Bien sûr, quelle taille ?

The shop assistant: Sure, what size are you?

Peter : L

Peter: Large.

La vendeuse : Malheureusement, nous n'avons que M et XL. **Voulez-vous essayer** celle-là ? Le modèle est similaire, et nous l'avons en L.

The shop assistant: Unfortunately, we only have it in Medium and XL. Would you like to try on this one? It is a similar model and we have it in Large.

Peter : Oui, pourquoi pas.

Peter: Yes, why not.

La vendeuse : Très bien. Les cabines d'essayage sont par là.

The shop assistant: Very well. The fitting rooms are over there.

Un peu plus tard :

A little later.

Peter : Elle est parfaite. Je la prends.

Peter: It is perfect, I will take it.

La vendeuse : Vous savez que nous faisons une réduction de 10% sur toute la collection homme ?

The shop assistant: You know we have 10% discount on all men's clothes?

Peter : Super ! Alors ça fait 55 euros, n'est-ce pas ?

Peter: That's great! So it is 55 euros, isn't it?

La vendeuse : Tout à fait. **Comment voulez-vous payer** ?

The shop assistant: Exactly. How would you like to pay?

Peter : Avec une carte de crédit, s'il vous plaît. Au fait, est-ce que vous avez un magasin en ligne ?

Peter: By credit card, please. By the way, do you have an online shop?

La vendeuse : Bien sûr. Voilà l'adresse du site.

The shop assistant: Of course. Here is our web site address.

Peter : Merci. Est-ce que la livraison est gratuite ?

Peter: Thanks. Is delivery free of charge?

La vendeuse : Oui, à condition que la commande soit supérieure à 100 euros.

The shop assistant: Yes, it is, as long as the order is over 100 euros.

Peter : OK, merci beaucoup. Au revoir.

Peter: OK, thank you very much. Bye.

USEFUL VOCABULARY : clothes, colors, money

- **Je peux vous aider ? Vous avez besoin d'aide** ? Can I help you? / Do you need any help?

- **Oui, s'il vous plaît, je cherche** ...Yes please, I am looking for ...

- **Non, merci, je regarde**. No, thanks, I am just looking.

Ça vous va bien. It suits you.

C'est la bonne taille. It fits you perfectly.

Excusez-moi, est-ce que vous pouvez m'aider ? Excuse me, can you help me, please?

Est-ce que vous avez cette chemise en M ? Do you have this shirt in medium?

Excusez-moi, je ne trouve pas le prix. Ça coûte combien ? Excuse me, I can't find the price. How much is it?

C'est en solde, à moitié prix. It's on sale. It's half price.

Où est-ce que je peux payer ? Where can I pay?

Les caisses sont par là. The cash desks are over there.

<u>Vêtements</u> – Clothes

mettre (un vêtement) – to put on ; **enlever** – to take off ; **la taille** – size

des vêtements homme – men's clothes ; **des vêtements femme** – ladies' clothes

une robe – dress ; **une jupe** – skirt ; une chemise – shirt ; **des manches longues** – long sleeves ; **manches courtes** – short sleeves

une veste – jacket ; **un pull** – sweater ; **un costume** – suit ; **un pantalon** – trousers; **un manteau** – coat ; **un imperméable** – raincoat ; **un bouton** – button

des sous-vêtements – underwear ; **un pyjama** – pyjamas ; **une nuisette** – night gown

des bas – tights ; **des chaussettes** – socks

des chaussures – shoes ; **des bottes** – boots ; **des escarpins** – high heels **des pantoufles** – slippers

<u>Des accessoires</u> – Accessories

un chapeau – hat ; **une cravate** – tie ; **un nœud papillon** – bow tie ; **une écharpe** – scarf ; **un sac à main** – handbag ; **une ceinture** – belt ; **des gants** – gloves ; **un parapluie** – umbrella ; **un porte-monnaie** – purse ; **un portefeuille** – wallet ; **une montre** – watch ; **des lunettes / lunettes de soleil** – glasses / sun glasses

Pour les bébés et les enfants – for babies and children

un berceau – cradle ; **un jouet** – toy ; **une poupée** – doll ; **un ballon** – ball ; **une poussette** – pram / stroller

la mode – fashion ; **à la mode** – fashionable

du tissu – fabrics ; **du coton** – cotton ; **de la laine** – wool ; **de la soie** – silk **du cuir** – leather ; **du lin** – linen ; **une rayure** – stripe ; **des carreaux** – check **un fil** – thread ; **une aiguille** – needle

<u>Les couleurs</u> – Colours

blanc – white ; **noir** – black ; **gris** – grey ; **marron** – brown ; **bleu** – blue ; **vert** – green **orange** – orange ; **jaune** – yellow ; **rouge** – red ; **rose** – pink ; **violet** – purple **coloré** – colourful ; **une couleur vive** – bright colour

<u>**Le style**</u> – Style

décontracté – casual ; **habillé** – formal ; **élégant** – smart / elegant **distingué,
chic** – stylish, chic

cher – expensive ; **bon marché** – cheap

<u>**Des bijoux**</u> – Jewellery

de l'argent – silver (and money!) ; **de l'or** – gold ; **un diamant** – diamond
des boucles d'oreille – earrings ; **un collier** – necklace ; **une chaîne** – chain
un bracelet – bracelet ; **une bague** – ring ; **une bague de fiançailles** – engagement ring
une alliance – wedding ring

<u>**La cosmétique**</u> – Cosmetics

un savon – soap ; **un vernis** – nail polish ; **un maquillage** – make-up ; **un rouge
à lèvres** – lipstick ; **un rouge** – blush ; **une teinture pour les cheveux** – hair dye
une laque pour les cheveux – hair spray ; **un rasoir** – razor
un après rasage – after shave

<u>**L'argent**</u> – Money

faire de l'argent – to make money ; **gagner** – to earn ; **acheter** – to buy ; **vendre** – to sell
payer – to pay ; **un salaire** – salary

<u>**La monnaie – Currency**</u>

un taux de change – exchange rate

des billets – notes ; **des pièces de monnaie** – coins ; **la monnaie** – change

Gardez la monnaie ! Keep the change!

du fric, des balles – bucks

une brique – grand

un compte bancaire – bank account ; **un compte d'épargne** – saving account
un compte courant – current account

un taux d'intérêt – interest rate

emprunter – to borrow ; **prêter** – to lend

un prêt – loan ; **une dette** – debt ; **endetté** – in debt

un emprunt immobilier – mortgage

retirer – to withdraw ; **virer, un virement** – to transfer ; **remplir un formulaire** – to
fill in a form ; **signer** – to sign ; **une signature** – signature

CHAPITRE 12

PREPOSITIONS

Prepositions are a difficult element in every language, not only in French. There are a few rules to guide you but in many cases you have to learn by heart which preposition goes with a particular verb or adjective. (see the Annex). The best way to get familiar to prepositions is **to read and to listen as much as possible**.

PREPOSITIONS OF PLACE
DANS, À, DE...

<u>dans</u> – in

DANS is most often used when we talk about something (or someone) situated in a closed space:

> **dans** le sac – in the bag
> **dans** la chambre – in the room
> **dans** le jardin – in the garden
>
> **dans** la rue – in the street
> **dans** le ciel – in the sky
> **dans** la queue – in a queue

<u>à</u> – **at / in / on**

With cities, some countries and places:

> à Los Angeles – in Los Angeles
> **aux** Etats-Unis – in the USA (aux = à + les)
>
> **à la** porte – at the door
> à l'arrêt du bus – at the bus stop
> à la maison – at home
> **au** travail – at work (au = à +le)
> à l'école – at school
> à l'université – at university

à l'aéroport – at the airport
à la fête – at a party
au match de football – at a football match
à la réunion – at a meeting

à la page 5 – **on** the 5th page
à gauche, à droite – **on** the left (right)

à côté de – next to, by
à l'extérieur – outside
à l'intérieur – inside
au coin de – in the corner of (au = à + le)

sur – on

sur la table – on the table
sur le mur – on the wall

sur la photo – in the photo

Other prepositions of **place**

chez

chez moi – at my place
chez le coiffeur – at the hairdresser's
chez Eugène – very often « chez » is combined with a person's name and
this is how a café or a restaurant is called

en

en France – in France
en haut de la page – at the top of the page
en bas de la page – at the bottom of the page

devant – in front of
en face de – opposite
derrière – behind
au-dessus de – above ; **au-dessous de** – below
par-dessus de – over ; **sous** – under
entre – between
près de – near

loin de – far from
au bord de – by

par (la fenêtre) – through (the window)
le long de – along
de l'autre côté de la rue – across the street
à travers – across
un voyage **à travers** l'Europe – a trip across Europe

PREPOSITIONS OF MOVEMENT
A, DE...

<u>à</u> – to

Especially with the verb « aller ».

aller **à la** banque – go to the bank
aller **à la** maison – go home
aller **au** travail – go to work (au = à + le)
aller à l'étranger – go abroad
aller **au** restaurant – go to a restaurant
aller **au** lit – go to bed

<u>de</u> – from

venir **de** – come back from

<u>en</u> – **by** (vehicle)
en voiture – by car ; **en avion** – by plane
en bus – by bus ; **en train** – by train
but : **à pied** – on foot ; **aller à pied** – go on foot / walk

<u>vers</u> – **to, toward / near**
vers le nord – to the north
vers Paris – near Paris

<u>par</u> – **by**

par mail – by email
par la poste – by post
Expressions with « **par** »:
par erreur – by mistake
par hasard – by chance

Other expressions of mouvement :

monter **dans** la voiture – get in the car

descendre **de** la voiture – get out of the car

monter **dans** un bus (train) – get on a bus or train

descendre **d**'un bus (train) – get off a bus or train

EXERCISES **Complete the gaps:**

1. - Où est-ce qu'ils habitent ? Where do they live?

- … Nashville. In Nashville.

…

2. - Comment vas-tu… l'école ? How do you go to school?

- D'habitude j'y vais … bus, et parfois je rentre … pied. I usually go by bus, and sometimes I walk on the way back.

…

3. – Mon mari rentre … la maison très tard. My husband gets home late in the evening.

- Mais il va … travail tard aussi, n'est-ce pas ? But he also goes to work late, doesn't he?

…

4. - Où es-tu ? Where are you?

- … travail. Et toi ? I am at work. And you?

- Moi, je suis … la maison I am at home.

…

5. - Tom arrive demain. Je vais le chercher … l'aéroport. Tom arrives tomorrow. I am going to meet him at the airport.

- Je peux venir moi aussi. I might come too.

…

6. - Tu veux qu'on aille … restaurant ce soir ? Je n'ai pas envie de faire la cuisine. Shall we go to a restaurant tonight? I don't feel like cooking.

- D'accord, je vais t'appeler dès que je finis le travail. OK, I will call you as soon as I finish work.

…

7. – Pourquoi la farine est ... la table ? Why is the flour on the table?

- Parce que je vais faire un gâteau. Because I'm going to make a cake.

...

8. - Où est-ce que tu veux t'asseoir ? Where would you like to sit?

- Je vais m'asseoir ... de toi. I'll sit next to you.

...

9. - Qui est l'homme ... cette photo ? Who is the man in this photo?

- Mon cousin. My cousin.

...

10. - J'ai rencontré Sylvie ... la rue hier. Yesterday I met Sylvie in the street.

- Comment va-t-elle ? How is she?

PREPOSITIONS of time : à, en, dans...

<u>à</u> – **at**

> **at** 8 o'clock – à 8 heures (time)
> **à l'heure** – on time
> **au** 19ème siècle – in the 19th century (centuries)

<u>en</u> – **in**

> **en** avril – in April (months)
> **en** 2000 – in 2000 (years)
> **en** été/ **en** automne / **en** hiver –in summer/autumn/winter (seasons)
> BUT : **au** printemps – in spring
> **en** ce moment – at the moment

<u>some expressions with **à** /**au** and **en**</u>

> **au** téléphone – on the phone
> **à la** télé – on the TV
> **à la** radio – on the radio
> **au** régime – on a diet
> **en** vacances – on holiday
> **en** voyage d'affaires – on a business trip
> **au** début de – at the beginning of
> **à** la fin de – at the end of

<u>**dans**</u> – **in**

> **dans** quelques minutes – in a few minutes
> **dans** une semaine – in a week

<u>**pendant**</u> – at, during, for

> **pendant** la nuit – at night
> **pendant** quelques années – for a few years (in the past)

<u>Other prepositions of **time**</u>

<u>**depuis**</u> – for, since

> **depuis** 2000 – since 2000
> **depuis** 5 years – for 5 years (until now)

<u>**de… à / jusqu'à**</u> – from…to/until

de 10 heures du matin **jusqu'à** 7 heures du soir – from 10am to 7pm.

<u>**avant**</u> – by, before

avant la fin du mois – by the end of the month

avant le concert – before the concert

<u>**après**</u> – after

après le show – after the show

<u>**environ**</u> une heure – about an hour

<u>**il y a**</u> – ago

il y a quelques jours – a few days ago

NO preposition

<u>1. Parts of the day</u>
le matin / l'après-midi / le soir – in the morning / in the afternoon / in the evening

<u>2. Days and dates</u>
lundi – on Monday

le 1er janvier – on 1st January

 Complete the gaps:

1. - Je suis né … avril. I was born in April.

- Quelle date ? What date?

- … 3 avril. On the 3rd of April.

…

2. - A quelle heure commence le film ? What time does the film start?

- … 8 heures, je pense. At 8 o'clock, I think.

…

3. - Est-ce qu'elle travaille ou elle reste à la maison avec les enfants ? Does she work or does she look after the children?

- Elle travaille à temps partiel, … 9 heures … 13 heures. She works part time, from 9am to 1pm.

…

4. - Je vais voir Laure…vendredi. I'm going to meet Laure on Friday.

- Dis-lui bonjour de ma part. Say hello to her for me.

…

5. Qu'est-ce qu'il se passe … la fin du film ? What happens at the end of the movie?

- Est-ce que tu veux vraiment savoir ? Do you really want to know?

…

6. - Où vas-tu ? Where are you going?

- Je vais … l'épicier. Je reviens … 5 minutes. To the grocery shop. I'll be back in 5 minutes.

…

7. - Est-ce que je peux vous parler maintenant ? Can I speak to you now?

- Je ne suis pas … bureau actuellement, je vais vous rappeler … environ une heure. Well, I am not at the office at the moment. I'll call you back in about an hour.

OTHER PREPOSITIONS

DE, POUR, AVEC, SANS…

<u>de</u> – about, of

parler, discuter de – talk, discuss about

il s'agit **de** – it is about

le sac **de** Pierre – Pierre's bag

la première page **du** livre – the first page of the book (du = de + le)

le centre **de** la ville – the centre of the city

trois tasses **de** café – three cups of coffee

décoration faite **de** bois – decoration made of wood

BUT : une robe **en** coton – a cotton dress

un grand nombre **de** personnes – a large number of people

une réduction **de** 10% – a discount of 10%

pour – for

c'est **pour** toi – this is for you

un gâteau **pour** ton anniversaire – a cake for your birthday

avec – with

Tu veux venir **avec** moi ? Do you want to come with me?

Il parle **avec** un léger accent irlandais. He speaks with a soft Irish accent.

sans – without

Je suis sorti **sans** parapluie. I went out without my umbrella.

Sans aucun doute il est l'un des meilleurs joueurs de tennis de tous les temps. Without any doubt he is one of the best tennis players of all time.

contre – against

une décision **contre** la loi – a decision against the law

parmi – among

selon – according to

Prepositions are an infinite topic. You will find some more useful expressions with an adjective or a verb followed by a preposition in the Annex. Fortunately, <u>there are no</u> phrasal verbs in French, which makes things easier ☺

EXERCISES — Complete the gaps:

1. - Parlez-moi ... votre projet. Talk to me about your project.

- Je vais vous montrer aussi quelques diapos. I will show you some slides as well.

...

2. - Il me semble que Caroline est amoureuse ... notre nouveau collègue. It seems to me that Caroline is in love with our new colleague.

- Tu crois ? Est-ce qu'elle n'a pas un petit ami ? Do you think so? Doesn't she have a boyfriend?

...

3. - Qu'est-ce qu'il y a ... la télé ce soir ? What is on TV tonight?

- Je ne sais pas, je dois voir. I don't know, I must check.

...

4. - Il est ... voyage d'affaires ... l'étranger. He is on a business trip abroad.

- Ah bon ? Où ça ? Is he? Where?

...

5. - Elle ne vient jamais ... bureau ... l'heure. She never arrives at work on time.

- C'est vrai, mais elle reste ... tard. It's true but she stays until late.

...

6. - Où allez-vous habituellement ... vacances d'été ? Where do you usually go on holiday in summer?

- ... Floride. To Florida.

...

7. - Ma meilleure amie aime parler ... téléphone, et moi, je déteste ! My best friend loves speaking on the phone, and I hate it!

- Pourquoi tu ne lui dis pas ? Why don't you tell her?

...

8. - Je t'attends ... une heure! Où es-tu? I have been waiting for you for one hour! Where are you?

- Je suis coincé ... un embouteillage. I am stuck in a traffic jam.

...

9. - Tu as parlé ... les voisins ... ce probleme? Did you talk to the neighbours about this problem?

- Oui, mais je ne suis pas satisfaite... leur réponse. Yes, but I am not happy with their answer.

...

10. - Nous devons choisir ... les deux options. We have to choose between the two options.

- Je vote pour la première ... hesitation. I vote for the first one without hesitation.

...

11. - Il y a des étudiants ... ceux qui protestent. There are students among those who are protesting.

- Ah bon? En fait, moi aussi je suis ... cette décision. Are there? In fact, me too, I am against this decision.

...

12. - ... la météo, il va pleuvoir demain. According to the weather forecast, it is going to rain tomorrow.

- Alors on ne pourra pas aller ... la plage. We won't be able to go to the beach then.

CHAPITER 13

ADJECTIVES AND ADVERBS

Adjectives always accompany the noun they describe, and in French they agree with the noun in gender (masculine or feminine) and in number (singular or plural).

un **grand** camion – a big truck

une **grande** ville – a big city

grands magasins – big shops

grandes maisons – big houses

grand: masculine; **grande**: feminine

grands: masculine plural; **grandes**: feminine plural

Adjective endings – les terminaisons des adjectifs

The masculine form of an adjective is its base form. As a general rule, the feminine form is made by adding an **-e**:

haut → haut**e**

petit → petit**e**

Attention to the prononciation!

Most adjectives in masculine form end in a consonnant which is not pronounced, but in the feminine form, with an added -e, it **is** pronounced!

Sometimes the masculine form already ends in **-e** and so both masculine and feminin forms are spelled and pronounced in the same way.

Examples:

célèbre – famous
facile – easy
drôle – funny
magnifique – wonderful
aimable – kind

There are some particularities in the formation of feminine adjectives, depending on how the masculine form ends:

Ending		Example		Translation
masculine	feminine	masculine	feminine	
-e	**-e**	jeune	jeune	young
-el	**-elle**	naturel	naturelle	natural
-eil	**-eille**	pareil	pareille	same
-en	**-enne**	ancien	ancienne	ancient
-on	**-onne**	bon	bonne	good
-er	**-ère**	léger	légère	light
-f	**-ve**	neuf	neuve	new
-c	**-che**	blanc	blanche	white

Adjectives which end in **-x**, **-et** or **-s** have irregular feminine forms. It is best to look up these words in the dictionary. Here are some examples:

-x	heur**eux**	heur**euse**	happy
	fau**x**	fau**sse**	wrong
	dou**x**	dou**ce**	soft
-et	net	ne**tte**	clear
	complet	compl**ète**	complete
-s	frai**s**	fra**îche**	fresh
	gra**s**	gra**sse**	fat

Pronunciation: In some of the examples above the ending of the feminine form introduces a new sound, like [ʃ] (the sound in « she ») in **blanche, fraîche** or [v] in **neuve** or [z] in **heureuse**.

👓 Exceptions

	masculine	feminine	translation
before a consonant	before a vowel or a „silent h"		
beau	**bel**	**belle**	beautiful
fou	**fol**	**folle**	crazy
nouveau	**nouvel**	**nouvelle**	new
vieux	**vieil**	**vieille**	old

Un beau garçon; un bel enfant; une belle femme

Adjectives which end in -ant and -é

They are similar to the English adjectives in -ing and -ed.

fatigant – fatigué ; tiring – tired

excitant – excité ; exciting – excited

ennuyant – ennuyé ; boring – bored

The adjectives ending in **-é** refer to people, while those in **-ant** to things.

The trip is « **fatigant** » (tiring), and you are « **fatigué** » (tired).

The book is « **ennuyant** » (boring), and you are « **ennuyé** » (bored).

The news is « **surprenante** » (surprising), and you are « **surpris** » (surprised).

Some adjectives in **-ant** can refer to people as well:

Elle est une **personne intéressante**. She is an interesting person.

Plural

The plural form (for both masculine and feminine) is made by adding the ending **-s**:

bon / bonne → bon**s** / bonne**s**

clair / claire → clair**s** / claire**s**

If the adjective in masculine ends in **-s** or **-x**, it does not change in plural :

un formage **français** → des fromages **français**

un étudiant **sérieux** → des étudiants **sérieux**

Exceptions

1. Most adjectives in masculine form which end in **-al**, get the ending -**aux** in plural, like **national, initial, spécial**, etc:

un cas spéci**al** → des cas spéci**aux**
un musée nation**al** → des musées nation**aux**

There are a few adjectives which end -al and do not change in plural, like **natal** (native) or **naval** (naval), but their use in plural is very rare.

un combat **naval** → des combats **navals**

2. Adjectives in masculine form which end in **-eau**, get the ending **-x** in plural, instead of -s:

beau → beau**x**
nouveau → nouveau**x**

Where to place the adjective?

In general, and unlike English, French adjectives are placed **after** the noun they describe :

une voiture chère – an expensive car
une robe élégante – an elegant dress
un gâteau délicieux – a delicious cake

However, some adjectives go **before** the noun, especially those referring to:

1. Opinion

beau/belle – beautiful
joli/jolie – pretty

bon/bonne – good
gentil/gentille – kind

une jolie femme – a pretty woman
un bon repas – a nice meal

2. Age

jeune – young
vieux/vielle – old

une vieille voiture – an old car
un jeune homme – a young man
BUT : des personnes âgées – elderly people

3. Size

petit(e) – small
haut(e) – high

une petite faute – a small mistake
une haute montagne – high mountain

Attention to the adjectives whose meaning changes depending on their position!

Adjective	Meaning **before** the noun	Meaning **after** a noun
ancien	*former* mon **ancienne** maison	*old* une maison **ancienne**
cher	*dear* mon **cher** ami	*expensive* une montre **chère**
drôle	*strange* une **drôle** d'histoire	*funny* une histoire **drôle**
grand (homme)	*great* un **grand** homme	*tall* un homme **grand**
pauvre	poor (pitiful) le **pauvre** homme	poor (without money) un homme **pauvre**
propre	*own* ma **propre** chambre	*clean* ma chambre **propre**

pur	*simple* une **pure** formalité	*pure, fresh* l'air **pur**
sacré	*awesome* un **sacré** livre	holy un livre **sacré**
vrai	real un **vrai** problème	true une histoire **vraie**

When there are two or more adjectives, they either « <u>frame</u> » the noun, or are put <u>before</u> the noun:

un **grand** ours **blanc** – a big white bear

de **longs** cheveux **noirs** – a long black hair

> Attention!
>
> Before an adjective in plural, the indefinite article « des » becomes « de »!

J'ai reçu **de** beaux cadeaux. I got some nice presents.

QUELQUES, CERTAINS, TOUT...
INDEFINITE ADJECTIVES

The indefinite adjectives are often used in everyday speech. They describe nouns in general or non-specific way.

<u>quelque /quelques</u> – some, a few

Je reviens dans **quelques** minutes. I am coming back in a few minutes.

<u>certain / certaine / certains</u> – some, certain

Certains étudiants s'intéressent au baseball. Some students are interested in baseball.

<u>tout/toute/tous/toutes</u> – all, every

Elle fait du yoga **tous les jours**. She does yoga every day.

Il a invité **tous ses amis**. He invited all his friends.

plusieurs – several

Ça n'a pas marché pour **plusieurs** raisons. It did not work for several reasons.

aucun, e – not any, without any

Elle s'est fâchée **sans aucune** raison. She got angry without any reason.

chaque – every

Ils se voient **chaque** semaine. They meet every week.

même / mêmes – same

Le contrat est fait sous **les mêmes** conditions. The contract is made under the same conditions.

ADVERBS
FORMATION, TYPES

What is the difference between an adjective and an adverb ?

Adjectives describe a noun, and adverbs describe a verb, sometimes even a whole sentence. Adverbs are **invariable** (no masculine, feminine, plural forms).

Michel est un chauffeur **prudent**. Michel is a careful driver.

Michel conduit **prudemment**. Michel drives carefully.

Many adverbs are formed directly from the adjective and have a typical ending **-ment** which is comparable to the English ending -ly.

HOW to make an adverb from an adjective ?

the **feminine form** of the adjective + **-ment**.

lent → lent**e** (fem.) → **lentement** – slow / slowly

attentif → attentiv**e** (fem.) → **attentivement** – careful / carefully

sérieux → sérieus**e** (fem.) → **sérieusement** – serious / seriously

Il est un homme **sérieux**. He is a serious person.

Il parle toujours **sérieusement**. He always speaks seriously.

Exceptions

1. Some adjectives whose masculine form ends in -e make their adverb with **-ément**.

    énorme → énorm**ément** – enormous/ enormously
    conforme → conform**ément** – in accordance with

2. Some adjectives whose masculine form ends in a vowel make their adverb by adding directly **-ment** (no need of the feminine form).

    vrai → vrai**ment** – real/really
    absolu → absolu**ment** – absolute/absolutely

3. Adjectives whose masculine form ends in **-ent** make an adverb with the ending -**emment**, and those in **-ant**, with **-amment**

récent	récemment	recent/recently
évident	évidemment	obvious/obviously
apparent	apparemment	apparent/apparently

constant	constamment	constant/constantly
courant	couramment	common/comonly/fluently
suffisant	suffisamment	enough
brillant	brillamment	brilliant/brilliantly

The pronounciation of both -**emment** and -**amment** is the same.

4. A few adjectives are completely **irregular** and have their own ways to make an adverb :

gentil	**gentiment**	kind/kindly
bref	**brièvement**	brief/briefly
bon	**bien**	good/well
mauvais	**mal**	bad/badly

A lot of adverbs are independent words which are not derived from an adjective. They can be classified in several groups:

Adverbs of **PLACE**

ici	here
là	there
dehors	outside
dedans	inside
loin	far
partout	everywhere
quelque part	somewhere
nulle part	nowhere

Adverbs of **TIME**

alors	then
hier	yesterday
aujourd'hui	today
demain	tomorrow
maintenant	now
souvent	often
toujours	always
parfois	sometimes
rarement	rarely
déjà	already
tout de suite	immediately
bientôt	soon
enfin	finally

Adverbs of **QUANTITY**

beaucoup	much/many
peu	little/few
très	very
trop	too much/many
assez	enough
davantage	more
plus	more
environ	about
mois	less/fewer
presque	almost
tant	so
tellement	so much/many

Adverbs of **AFFIRMATION / DOUBT**

assurément	certainly
certainement	definitely
bien sûr	of course
précisément	exactly
probablement	probably
peut-être	perhaps
sans doute	without a doubt
vraiment	truly

Adverbs of **NEGATION**

jamais	never
rien	nothing
pas du tout	not at all

The negative adverbs « **jamais** » and « **rien** » replace « pas » in a negative sentence:

Il ne boit pas de café. He does not drink coffee.

Il ne boit **jamais** de café. He never drinks coffee.

Je n'ai pas entendu de bruit. I did not hear any noise.

Je n'ai **rien** entendu. I did not hear anything.

Position of adverbs in a sentence

The general rule is that adverbs come <u>**after**</u> the verb they are describing (and after the auxilliary verb in compound verb tenses).

Il chante **bien**. He sings well.

Il a **bien** chanté. He sang well.

Adverbs of <u>time</u> are often placed at the beginning or at the end of the sentence:

Hier j'ai beaucoup travaillé. Yesterday I worked hard.

or J'ai beaucoup travaillé **hier**.

Parfois elle invite ses amis à dîner. Sometimes she invites her friends for dinner.

Attention!

Adverbs are never placed after the subject, as it is often the case in English!

Je fais **toujours** mes devoirs. I always do my homework. (not ~~Je toujours fais mes devoirs~~)

Nous allons **souvent** au cinéma. We often go to the cinema. (not ~~Nous souvent allons au cinéma.~~)

In order to get familiar with adverbs and their position in the sentence, you should read in French and listen to French as much as possible.

COMPARATIVES and SUPERLATIVES

Comparison in French is easier than in English. There is only one way to make the comparative form, and it does not depend on whether the adjective (or the adverb) is short or long.

Comparative

Plus ....**que** – more ...... than
Moins .....**que** – less .... than
Aussi ......**que** – as .... as

jeune	**plus** jeune	young /younger
raisonnable	**plus** raisonnable	reasonable/more reasonable
intéressant	**plus** intéressant	interesting/more interesting
vite	**plus** vite	fast / faster

Le japonais est **plus difficile que** le français. Japanese is more difficult than French.

Il ne parle pas **aussi fort que** moi. He does not speak as loud as me.

Cette voiture est **moins confortable que** la mienne. This car is less comfortable than mine.

In order to be more expressive, we can add <u>beaucoup</u>, <u>un peu</u>, <u>même</u>:

    beaucoup plus grand – a lot bigger
    un peu moins cher – a bit less expensive
    même plus intéressant – even more interesting

We can also compare <u>nouns</u> and <u>verbs</u> :

Nouns: **plus de / moins de / autant de**

Verbs: **plus que / moins que / autant que**

J'ai **plus de** travail maintenant. I have more work now.

Je travaille **plus qu**'avant. I work more than before.

Il y a **moins de** monde dans les rues ces jours-ci. There are fewer people in the streets these days.

Superlative

The superlative form depends on the gender and the number of the adjective.

<u>The most</u>

> Masculine: **Le plus**
> Feminine: **La plus**
> Plural: **Les plus**
>
> **le plus cher** marché – the most expensive market
> **la plus chère** voiture – the most expensive car
> **les plus chers** produits – the most expensive products
>
> **la plupart des gens** – most people
> **la plupart du temps** – most of the time

<u>The least</u>

> Masculine: **Le moins**
> Feminine: **La moins**
> Plural: **Les moins**

<u>Exceptions</u>

bon	meilleur	le meilleur
bien	mieux	le mieux
mauvais	plus mauvais/pire	le plus mauvais/le pire
petit	plus petit/moindre	le plus petit/le moindre
beaucoup	plus	le plus
peu	moins	le moins

Strong adjectives

Some adjectives are strong enough and cannot have a comparative form. You cannot say « more wonderful » in English nor « plus magnifique » in French.

Most « base » adjectives have strong synonyms, and it would be useful for you to learn them. It will help you enrich your vocabulary and make it more vivid, colourful and impressive.

Here is a list of some commonly used strong adjectives:

intéressant	interesting	**fascinant** **incroyable**	fascinating amazing
beau, belle	beautiful	**ravissant**	gorgeous
joli	nice	**magnifique** **merveilleux**	wonderful lovely
bon	good	**superbe** **génial** **fantastique** **excellent**	superb great fantastic excellent
mauvais	bad	**terrible** **horrible**	terrible awful
heureux	happy	**ravi**	thrilled
bon au goût	tasty	**délicieux**	delicious
drôle	funny	**hilarant**	hilarious
grand	big	**énorme**	huge
petit	small	**minuscule**	tiny
fâché	angry	**furieux**	furious
fatigué	tired	**extenué**	exhausted
froid	cold	**glacial**	freezing
chaud	hot	**brûlant**	boiling

EXERCISES — Complete the gaps:

1. - Pourquoi vas-tu à la campagne ... weekends ? Why do you go to the country every weekend?

- C'est ... là-bas. Beaucoup ... qu'en ville. It is wonderful there. Much better than in the city.

...

2. - Il est ... intelligent. He is exceptionally clever.

- Oui, c'est vrai. Et il est une ... personne en plus. Yes, he is. And he is a good person too.

...

3. - Est-ce que vous pouvez parler ..., s'il vous plaît ? Je ne vous comprends pas. Could you speak louder please? I cannot understand you.

- **Oui, bien sûr.** Yes, of course.

...

4. - Real Madrid a vraiment … joué hier soir. Real Madrid played really well last night.

- **Hm, moi je ne pense pas qu'ils etaient … que Liverpool, tout simplement ils ont eu de la chance.** Hm, I don't think they were better than Liverpool, they were just lucky.

...

5. - J'aime ce restaurant. Les plats sont toujours …. I love this restaurant. The food is always delicious.

- **Je dois te montrer un nouveau, pas …. Il n'est pas … cher, et ils ont du vin excellent.** I must show you a new one nearby. It isn't so expensive, and they have an excellent wine list.

...

6. - La prononciation en français est difficile. Pronunciation in French is difficult.

- **Oui, c'est vrai, mais je pense qu'en anglais elle est … difficile.** Yes, it is, but I think in English it is even more difficult.

...

7. – Quelle compagnie est votre partenaire en affaires … ? Which company is your closest business partner?

- **Ce n'est pas une seule, il y en a plusieurs qui sont proches.** There isn't only one, there are several which are close.

DIALOGUE   « Talking about family »

Peter and Olivier are talking one day about their families.

Olivier : Dis, tu as une grande famille ?	Olivier : Tell me, do you have a big family?
Peter : Pas très grande, mais quand même – nous sommes trois enfants, j'ai deux sœurs, une plus jeune et une plus âgée que moi.	Peter : Not very big but still we are three children – I have two sisters, one younger, and one older than me.
Olivier : Ça doit être bien d'avoir des sœurs… moi, j'ai deux frères.	Olivier : It must be cool to have sisters… I have two brothers.
Peter : Est-ce que tu ne t'entends pas bien avec eux ?	Peter : Don't you get on well with them?
Olivier : Si, surtout avec mon frère aîné, il est tolérant et facile à vivre avec.	Olivier : Yes, I do, especially with my elder brother. He is tolerant and easy-go-

En plus nous avons pas mal d'intérêts communs. En revanche, le cadet est un peu trop égocentrique, il croit que le monde tourne autour de lui.

Peter : Oui, je comprends... Mais tu sais, au moins avec les garçons on a toujours des sujets communs à discuter, et moi avec mes sœurs, ce n'est pas aussi facile. Elles sont charmantes et affectueuses toutes les deux, mais elles s'intéressent à la mode et à des choses de ce type que je trouve ennuyantes. Heureusement que ma sœur cadette aime le sport comme moi. Elle est un peu têtue, mais je suis habitué. D'ailleurs, elle va probablement venir à Paris le mois prochain.

Olivier : Super, tu vas lui acheter des robes Dior et Channel ! ☺

Peter : Penses-tu !

ing. We also have a lot of common interests. But the younger one is a bit too egocentric. He believes that the world turns around him.

Peter : Yes, I see... But you know, at least with the boys you always have things to discuss, and with my sisters it is not so easy. They are both lovely and affectionate but they are interested in fashion and the sort of things which I find boring. Fortunately my younger sister loves sport like me. She is a bit stubborn, but I am used to it. By the way, she will probably come to Paris next month.

Olivier : Great, you will buy her some dresses Dior and from Channel! ☺

Peter : You think so?

USEFUL VOCABULARY: Describing a person

<u>Décrire une personne – Describing a person</u>

Comment est-il/elle (physiquement) ?What does he look like?

Il/elle est...He/she is...

petit, e – short ; **grand, e** – tall

mince – slim ; **large, corpulent,e** – large, chubby

belle – beautiful ; **jolie** – pretty; **adorable** – gorgeous

beau (pour un homme) – handsome

beau, belle – good looking

séduisant, e; attrayant, e – attractive

charmant, e – charming

mignon, ne – cute

jeune – young

un fils cadet / une fille cadette – younger son / daughter

un fils aîné / une fille aînée – elder son / daughter

un frère aîné / une sœur aînée – elder brother / sister

le cadet, la cadette – the youngest ; **l'aîné, l'aînée** – the eldest

<u>Cheveux (plural noun!)</u> – hair

bruns, marrons – brown ; **noirs** – black ; **blonds** – blonde

bouclés – curly ; **lisses** – sraight

courts – short ; **longs** – long

une barbe – beard ; **des moustaches** – moustache

une peau claire – fair skin ; **une peau brune** – dark skin

d'âge moyen – middle-aged

âgé, e – elderly ; **vieux, vieille** – old

<u>Décrire la personnalité – Describing personality</u>

Comment est-il/elle ? (comme personne) What is she like?

Il/elle est... He/she is...

Special attention to the pronunciation of those adjectives which have the same (or almost the same) spelling as the English words but are pronounced in a different way! If you apply the rules from Unit 1, you will pronounce them correctly.

magnifique – lovely ; **adorable** – adorable

serviable, aimable – helpful ; **compréhensif, ve** – understanding

charmant, e ; charismatique – charming, charismatic ; **sociable** – sociable
gentil, gentille – friendly, kind ; **optimiste** – upbeat

courageux, euse – brave ; **audacieux, euse** – daring ; **ouvert(e) d'esprit** – open-minded ; **tolérant, e** – tolerant ; **distrait, e** – absent-minded

ambitieux, euse – ambitious ; **travailleur, euse** – hard-working ; **sûr(e) de soi** – self-confident ; **compétent,e** – competent ; **persévérant, e** – persevering
appliqué, e – diligent ; **têtu, e ; obstiné, e** – stubborn

affectueux, euse – affectionate ; **poli(e), aimable** – polite ; **calme** – calm
désintéressé, e – selfless ; **prudent(e)** – careful / cautious

impulsif, ve – impulsive ; **autoritaire** – bossy ; **égoïste** – selfish ; **agressif, ve** – aggressive ; **impoli, e** – rude –; **tricheur, se** – cheat

sans scrupules – unscrupulous ; **avare, radin(e)** – mean ; **gourmand(e), avide** – greedy

insolent – cheeky

ennuyeux, se – boring ; **timide** – shy ; **anxieux, euse** ; **inquiet(e)** – anxious
paresseux, euse – lazy ; **curieux, euse** – curious

extraverti(e) – outgoing ; **drôle** – funny ; **bavard(e)** – talkative ; **réservé(e)** – reserved

intelligent(e), habile – Intelligent / clever ; **créatif, ve** – creative ; **plein d'esprit** – witty ; **observateur, trice** – observant

honnête – honest ; **modeste** – modest ; **fier, e** – proud ; **fiable** – reliable

stupide, bête – stupid / silly

Tu fais des bêtises ! (informal) You are being silly!

Tu fais l'intéressant. (ironic) You're being smart!

CHAPTER 14

PASSÉ COMPOSÉ

Translated in English by **Past Simple** (I worked) or **Present Perfect** (I have worked)

«Passé composé » is similar in its form to Present Perfect (auxiliary verb plus past participle) but it corresponds to **Past Simple** and, in many cases, to **Present Perfect**. Two English tenses = one French.

HOW do we form it?

> **AVOIR (ou être) + participe passé**

In most cases **AVOIR** is the auxiliary (helping) verb. Let's look again at its conjugation.

j'ai	nous avons
tu as	vous avez
il/elle a	ils/elles ont

Le participe passé (past participle) has different endings depending on the type of the verb.

Verbs I group

-é

parler → **parlé**

regarder → **regardé**

J'ai regardé le match hier soir. I watched the match last night.

Nous avons parlé ce matin. We talked this morning.

Verbs II group

-i

réussir → **réussi**

choisir → **choisi**

Ils ont choisi une petite maison. They chose (have chosen) a small house.

Verbs III group

This is the group of the **irregular verbs**.

The past participles and the conjugation in *Passé composé* of the two main verbs **avoir** and **être**:

avoir → **eu**

être → **été**

avoir

I/you/he/she… had

j'ai eu	nous avons eu
tu as eu	vous avez eu
il/elle a eu	ils/elles ont eu

être

I//he/she was; we/you/they were

j'ai été	nous avons été
tu as été	vous avez été
il/elle a été	ils/elles ont été

Nous avons eu beaucoup de problèmes avec cette commande. We had a lot of problems with this order.

Il a été directeur pendant cinq ans. He was a manager for five years.

Most participles of irregular verbs end in **-u**, but some in **-it, -is, -ert**.

boire /to drink	**bu**	**connaitre** / to know	**connu**
devoir /must	**dû**	**croire** / to believe	**cru**
lire / to read	**lu**	**plaire** / to be liked	**plu**
pouvoir /can	**pu**	**recevoir** /to receive	**reçu**

savoir / to know	su	vendre / to sell	vendu
vivre /to live	vécu	voir / to see	vu
vouloir /to want	voulu		

construire / to build	construit	dire / to say	dit
écrire / to write	écrit	faire / to do	fait
mettre / to put	mis	ouvrir / to open	ouvert
prendre /to take	pris		

All these verbs are conjugated in the Present in Unit 4, and you will find there some other verbs with similar conjugation. These similar verbs make their past participles in the same way. For example:

mettre → **mis** similar: admettre – **admis,** permettre – **permis**

ouvrir → **ouvert** similar: couvrir – **couvert**, offrir – **offert**

vendre → **vendu** similar: attendre – **attendu**, entendre – **entendu**

J'ai lu beaucoup de romans américains. I have read a lot of American novels.

Il a écrit un long rapport. He wrote (has written) a long report.

Ils ont fait des travaux de rénovation l'année passée. They did some renovation work last year.

Impersonal verbs **il faut** and **il pleut**

il faut / must	il a fallu / had to
il pleut / it is raining	il a plu / it rained
il neige / it is snowing	il a neigé / it snowed

Il a plu toute la nuit. It rained all night long.

Il a fallu reporter le tournoi. The tournament had to be postponed.

Verbs which require ETRE as auxiliary

A few verbs make *le Passé composé* with the auxiliary **être**.

je suis	nous sommes
tu es	vous êtes
il/elle est	ils/elles sont

1. <u>14 verbs</u>, most of which express movement. They can be grouped in couples to make learning easier. Each couple is made of two verbs of movement with opposite meaning.

aller / venir	to go / to come
arriver / partir	to arrive / to leave
entrer / sortir	to come in / to go out
monter / descendre	to go up / to go down
tomber / rester	to fall / to stay
passer / retourner	to go by / to go back
naitre / mourir	to be born / to die

aller	**allé**	venir	**venu**
arriver	**arrivé**	partir	**parti**
entrer	**entré**	sortir	**sorti**
monter	**monté**	descendre	**descendu**
tomber	**tombé**	rester	**resté**
passer	**passé**	retourner	**retourné**
naître	**né**	mourir	**mort**

Attention!

When a verb takes être as auxiliary, the past participle always agrees in gender and number with the subject. You have to add -e (feminine) or -s (plural masculine) / -es (plural feminine).

Je suis **allé(e)**	nous sommes **allé(e)s**
Tu es **allé(e)**	vous êtes **allé(e)s**
Il est **allé**	ils sont **allés**
Elle est **allée**	elles sont **allées**

Ils sont arrivés il y a quelques jours. They arrived a few days ago.

Elle est partie à Cuba. She's gone to Cuba.

Attention!

Some verbs of this group take **avoir** when they are used with a direct object, for example **descendre quelque chose** (to bring something down), **sortir quelque chose** (to take something out).

Il a sorti les valises de la voiture. He took the suitcases out of the car.

2. All pronominal (reflexive) verbs

We studied the reflexive pronouns and the Present of pronominal verbs in Unit 4. To make *le Passé composé* you need the auxiliary **être** and the past participle.

Example:

se laver

je me suis lavé(e)	nous nous sommes lavé(e)s
tu t'es lavé(e)	vous vous êtes lavé(e)s
il s'est lavé	ils se sont lavés
elle s'est lavée	elles se sont lavées

In most cases the past participle <u>agrees</u> in gender and number with the subject:

Elle s'est levée tôt ce matin. She got up early this morning.

However, the past participle does not agree with the subject in the following cases:

– If the verb is followed by a direct object (with no preposition)

Elle s'est lavé les mains. She washed her hands.

Elle s'est rendu compte de son erreur. She realized her mistake.

– With verbs like **se parler**, **se téléphoner**, because the reflexive pronoun here is an indirect object (meaning « each other »):

Ils se sont parlé longtemps. They talked to each other for a long time.

Attention! **ON = nous**

On, which often replaces **nous** in spoken French, is always conjugated like 3 person singular (like il/elle), but in *Passé composé* with **être**, the past participle is in plural form.

On est allés à la plage hier. We went to the beach yesterday.

On s'est rencontrés dans un bar. We met in a bar.

<u>Agreement</u> of the past participle when the auxiliary is <u>**avoir**</u>

For verbs that take **avoir** in *Passé composé*, the past participle does not agree in gender and number with the subject.

Elle a mangé un hamburger. She had a hamburger.

Ils ont regardé le football ensemble. They watched the football together.

However, the participle has to agree with a <u>**direct object**</u> if this object is placed <u>**before the verb**</u>.

Direct object in a sentence is something (or someone) that does not perform the action and there is no preposition before. For example:

Ils ont acheté <u>la voiture</u>. They bought the car. (no agreement of the past participle)

> « La voiture » is a direct object and if we replace it with the pronoun « la », the sentence will become:

Ils **l'**ont **achetée**. They bought it. (l'ont = la ont)

Here we have to make the agreement because there is a direct object <u>before</u> the verb. In this case the object is feminine **(la)** so we add **-e**.

Ils ont acheté les cadeaux. They bought the presents.

Ils **les** ont **achetés**. They bought them. **(les** – masculine, plural so we add **-s)**

Il m'a donné une robe. He gave me a dress.

C'est **la robe** qu'il m'a **donnée**. This is the dress he gave me.

The direct object (« la robe ») is before the verb in the second sentence, so we have to make an agreement.

(-) <u>Negative form</u>

ne... pas

The negative sentence is made, as always, with **ne...pas**, which « frame » the auxiliary **avoir** or **être**.

Je **n'ai pas** parlé avec le professeur. I did not talk to the teacher.

Il **n'a pas** répondu au mail. He did not answer the email.

Le train **n'est pas** arrivé à temps. The train did not arrive on time.

Ils **ne sont pas sortis** hier soir. They did not go out last night.

<u>Word order with pronominal verbs</u>:

If the verb is pronominal, the particle « ne » is placed <u>before</u> the reflexive pronoun <u>me</u>, <u>te</u>, <u>se</u>....

Je **ne me suis pas** couché(e) tôt. I did not go to bed early.

Elle **ne s'est pas** fâchée. She did not get angry.

Ils **ne se sont pas** inquiétés. They did not worry.

(?) <u>Question form</u>

The three usual ways to make a question:

1. Est-ce que...

Est-ce que tu as répondu au mail ? Did you answer the mail?

2. Intonation (rising at the end)

Tu as lu ce livre ? Have you read that book ?

3. Inversion

Avez-vous rempli le formulaire ? Did you fill in the form?

(- ?) **Negative question**

Est-ce que tu n'as pas demandé au professeur ? Didn't you ask the teacher?

Tu n'es pas allé à la fête ? Didn't you go to the party?

Possible answers:

Je n'y suis pas allé. No, I didn't.

Si, j'y suis allé. Yes, I did.

« **Si** » replaces « oui » as a possible answer to a negative question.

N'est-ce pas ?

Didn't you? Did you? Didn't he? Did he?

Tu as parlé avec le manager, **n'est-ce pas** ? You talked to the manager, didn't you?

Elle ne t'a pas donné le livre, **n'est-ce pas** ? She didn't give you the book, did she?

Passé composé of **IL Y A**

Il y a eu – there was / there were

(?) Est-ce qu'il y a eu?

(-) Il n'y a pas eu...

Est-ce qu'il y a eu des annonces importantes? Was there any important news?

Il n'y a pas eu beaucoup de passagers sur ce vol. There were not many passengers on this flight.

WHEN
do we use le **Passé composé**?

Le Passé composé is equivalent to Past Simple, and to Present Perfect (in most cases).

<u>– Equivalent to Past Simple</u>
When we talk about actions or situations in the past.

Il a commencé ces cours il y a deux mois. He started this course two_months ago.

Ils se sont rencontrés l'année dernière. They met last year.

Elle est arrivée hier. She arrived yesterday.

<u>– Equivalent to Present Perfect</u>

1. When we talk about a <u>past action, connected with the present</u>.

Il **a été** au Japon. He has been to Japan.

Il **a perdu** son passeport. He has lost his passport.

2. Questions with « <u>déjà</u> » (ever)

Est-ce que tu as (déjà) **goûté** la cuisine japonaise ? Have you (ever) tried Japanese food?

Est-ce que tu as (déjà) **été** en Angleterre ? Have you (ever) been to England?

Tu as vu le film « The big short » ? Have you seen the film « The big short »?

3. When we talk about periods which are <u>not finished yet</u>.

Je n'ai pas vu Tom ce matin. I have not seen Tom this morning.

Nous ne sommes pas allés en vacances cette année. We have not been on holiday this year.

Le passé récent

Translated in English by **Present Perfect** (have **just** done).

This past verb tense, very easy to form, is commonly used in everyday speech when we talk about something which has just happened.

It is made with the verb « **venir** » which is the auxiliary, and the infinitive of the main verb:

> **venir + de + infinitif**

je viens	nous venons
tu viens	vous venez
il/elle vient	ils/elles viennent

Je viens de rentrer à la maison. I have just come back home.

Elle vient de m'appeler. She has just called me.

Nous venons de dîner. We have just had dinner.

or **On vient de** dîner. (on = nous, conjugated like 3rd person, singular)

It is most often used in affirmative form, and rarely in question or negative form.

Le Passé Simple

Le **Passé Simple** is another past tense, which has exactly the same meaning as **Passé composé**. It is no longer used in modern spoken French but you will find it in all classic literature and even in many contemporary books and articles.

Examples:

> **être** – je fus, tu fus, il fut, nous fûmes, vous fûtes, ils furent
> **avoir** – j'eus, tu eus, il eut, nous eûmes, vous eûtes, ils eurent
> **aller** – j'allai, tu allas, il alla, nous allâmes, vous allâtes, ils allèrent
> **faire** – je fis, tu fis, il fit, nous fîmes, vous fîtes, ils firent.

EXERCISES   Conjugate the verbs:

1. - Est-ce que tu ... (regarder) le baseball hier soir ? Did you watch the baseball last night?

- Oui, je .... (regarder). C'est dommage qu'on .... (ne pas gagner). Yes, I watched it. Such a pity we did not win.

...

2. - Est-ce que vous ... (discuter) du nouveau produit pendant le workshop ? Did you discuss the new product at the workshop?

- Non. Nous ... (parler) des problèmes de livraison. No, we didn't. We talked again about the delivery problems.

...

3. - Pourquoi tu ... (ne pas envoyer) la présentation ? Why didn't you send me the presentation slides?

- Je... (oublier), désolé. I forgot, sorry.

...

4. - Tu ...(être) en Grèce ? Have you been to Greece?

- Oui, ...(être). Il y a deux ans on...(aller) en vacances à Thessaloniki. Yes, I have. Two years ago we went on holiday to Thessaloniki.

...

5. - Tu ... (avoir) faim ? Are you hungry?

- Non, je ...(ne pas avoir) faim. Je ....(déjeuner). No, I'm not. I have just had lunch.

...

6. - Quand est-ce que ton ami des Etats Unis ...(arriver) ? When did your friend from the USA arrive?

- Lundi. Il ...(rester) à Londres quelques jours avant de venir ici. On Monday. He stayed in London for a few days before that.

...

7. - Est-ce que tu ...(faire) la réservation pour le restaurant ? Have you made a booking for the restaurant?

- Non, pas encore. Je vais les appeler plus tard. No, not yet. I'll call them later.

...

8. - Comment va Max ? Je ...(ne pas voir) depuis une éternité. How is Max? I haven't seen him for ages.

- Il va bien. Mais il ... (ne pas aimer) son travail, et il ...(chercher) un nouveau. He is fine. But he doesn't like his job and he is looking for a new one.

...

9. - Combien de temps vous …(vivre) en Allemagne avant de déménager en France ? How long did you live in Germany before you moved to France?

- Cinq ans, mais après on …(être) en Angleterre pour environ une année. For five years, but after that we were in England for about a year.

…

10. - Est-ce que tu …(écrire) la proposition ? Have you written the proposal yet?

- Non, je ne l'ai pas encore écrite. No, I haven't.

- Qu'est-ce que tu …(faire) tout l'après- midi ? What are you doing all afternoon?

- Je …(calculer) les dépenses. I am calculating the expenses.

DIALOGUE « Visit in a museum »

Peter invites Julie to an exposition in the museum Grand Palais.

Peter : Salut, Julie, comment vas-tu ?

Peter: Hi Julie, how are you today?

Julie : Ça va bien, et toi ?

Julie: Fine, thanks, and you?

Peter : Très bien, merci. Tu sais qu'il y a une exposition de Edward Hopper ce mois au Grand Palais ? **J'ai vu** beaucoup de ses tableaux sur Internet, et **j'ai toujours eu** envie de voir les originaux. Tu veux qu'on aille ensemble ce samedi ?

Peter: Very well, thank you. Do you know that there is an exhibition of Edward Hopper in Grand Palais this month? I have seen many of his paintings on the Internet and I have always wanted to see the originals. Why don't we go together this Saturday?

Julie : Hm, ça semble très intéressant. J'avais l'intention de rendre visite à ma tante samedi, mais ce n'est pas urgent. Je peux reporter à dimanche.

Julie: Hm, sounds very interesting. I was going to visit my aunt on Saturday, but it is not urgent. I can go on Sunday.

Peter : Alors tu viens avec moi ? Super ! Je dois réserver les billets en ligne, n'est-ce pas ?

Peter: So you are coming with me? Great! I should book the tickets online, shouldn't I?

Julie : Ah oui, absolument! Sinon, on va attendre pendant des heures. Quand tu réserves en ligne, ils précisent un intervalle de temps, et en plus, la queue est séparée et bouge très vite .

Julie: Oh yes, absolutely! Otherwise, we will be waiting for hours. When you book online, they give you a time interval, plus, the queue is separated and moves very quickly.

Peter : Alors je fais ça et je t'appelle pour te dire à quelle heure il faut y aller. Je vais venir te chercher en voiture.

Peter: So I am going to do this and will call you to say what time we need to be there. I'll come to pick you up.

Julie : Parfait ! A samedi alors !

Julie: Perfect! See you on Saturday then!

They are talking in the car on the way to the museum:

Peter : **J'ai vu** Le Hobbit: La Bataille des cinq armées, hier soir. **Tu l'as vu** ?

Peter: I saw The Hobbit: the Battle of the five armies last night. Have you seen it?

Julie : Non, **je ne l'ai pas vu**, mais **j'ai lu** le livre. Il est génial. Tu as aimé le film ?

Julie: No, I haven't, but I have read the book. It is great. Did you like the movie?

Peter : **Je l'ai beaucoup aimé** ! Et les acteurs sont superbes. Tu dois le voir.

Peter: I loved it! And the actors are brilliant! You must see it.

Julie : D'accord, je vais le voir. Mais parfois on est déçu quand on regarde un film après avoir lu le livre.

Julie: Yes, I will. But sometimes you are disappointed when you see a film after you have read the book.

Peter : C'est vrai. Un livre procure toujours plus. Mais le cinéma a son propre charme.

Peter: That's right. A book always gives you more. But cinema has its own charm.

Julie : Oui... surtout quand il y a des effets visuels et une belle musique. En parlant de musique, quel est ce groupe ? Il me plaît.

Julie: Yes... especially when there are visual effects and nice music. Talking about music, what is this band? I like it.

Peter : Muse. Ils sont bons, n'est-ce pas ?

Peter: Muse. They are great, aren't they?

USEFUL VOCABULARY : books, music, cinéma

<u>Livres</u> – <u>Books</u>

If you like reading, it means you have one more precious tool to improve your French. You can start with some easy short stories or adapted novels.

un auteur – author ; **un écrivain** – writer ; **un traducteur** – translator **un éditeur** – publisher ; **un personnage** – character ; **le personnage principal** – the main character ; **un roman** – novel ; **une nouvelle** – short story **un roman policier** – detective story ; **un manuel** – textbook ; **un livre de**

cuisine – cook book ; **un marque-page** – bookmark ; **un signet** – bookmark (computer)

une bibliothèque – library ; **emprunter un livre de la bibliothèque** – to borrow a book from the library

Est-ce que tu lis ? Do you read?

Est-ce que tu as lu « Le portrait de Dorian Grey » ? Have you read "The Picture of Dorian Gray"?

Qu'est-ce que tu lis en ce moment ? What are you reading?

Je lis un livre très intéressant d'un jeune auteur français. I am reading a very interesting book by a young French writer.

C'est quoi l'histoire ? What is it about?

<u>Musique</u> – Music

You can learn a lot from song lyrics. Search some videos of French singers and bands in your favourite style with the lyrics on screen and enjoy!

un goût musical – musical taste ; **une chanson** – song ; **le texte d'une chanson** – lyrics ; **un hymne national** – national anthem ; **un compositeur** – composer ; **un chanteur, une chanteuse** – singer ; **un chef d'orchestre** – conductor

des écouteurs – earphones ; **des haut-parleurs** – speakers ; **le son** – sound **fort** – loud ; **augmenter le son** – to turn up ; **diminuer le son** – to turn down **mettre sur le marché** – to release ; **une chanson** – single ; **un disque** – record **écouter de la musique** – to listen to music ; **faire jouer une chanson** – to play a song ; **jouer du piano /de la guitare** – to play the piano/the guitar ; **danser** – to dance

Tu aimes écouter de la musique ? Do you like listening to music?

Quel genre de musique tu aimes ? What kind of music do you like?

Est-ce que tu vas souvent aux concerts ? Do you often go to a concert?

Tu sais que Shakira a sorti un nouvel album ? Do you know that Shakira has released a new album?

<u>Cinéma</u> – cinema

un film – film / movie ; **un réalisateur** – director ; **une vedette du cinéma** – movie star ; **jouer dans un film** – to star
Est-ce que tu aimes les films d'horreur ? Do you like horror movies?

Qui joue dans ce film ? Who stars in this film?

Qui est ton acteur préféré ? Who is your favourite actor?

Est-ce que tu as vu « Grand Budapest Hotel » ? Have you seen « Grand Budapest Hotel »?

des beaux-arts – fine art ; **un tableau** – painting ; **un peintre** – painter **une exposition** – exhibition

DIALOGUE « About la tartiflette and other delicious things »

After the museum they are going to a small restaurant in Quartier Latin.

Peter : Qu'est que tu vas boire ?

Peter: What would you like to drink?

Julie : Je vais prendre une bière. Et toi ?

Julie: I'll have a beer. And you?

Peter : Moi aussi. Peut-être un peu de fromage en accompagnement ? J'ai entendu dire que vous avez beaucoup de sortes de fromage.

Peter: Me too. What about a bit of cheese to go with it? I've heard you have a lot of kinds of cheese.

Julie : Tu sais, notre président Charles de Gaulle avait dit une fois : « Comment voulez-vous gouverner un pays qui a deux cent quarante-six variétés de fromage ? »

Julie: You know what our president Charles de Gaulle said once : « How can you govern a country which has two hundred and forty six varieties of cheese? ».

Peter : Non ! Vous ne pouvez pas avoir autant !

Peter: No! You cannot have so many!

Julie : Pour te dire la vérité, il y en a même plus, peut-être plus de 400. Je ne pense pas que j'ai tout goûté, mais j'ai quelques favoris et plats préférés. Par exemple, la tartiflette, c'est fait à base de pommes de terre, lardons, oignons, un peu de vin, et bien sûr, du fromage français particulier.

Julie: To tell you the truth, there are even more, probably more than 400. I don 't think I have tasted everything but I have some favourite varieties and dishes. For example, tartiflette, which is made of potatoes, bacon, onion, a bit of wine, and some special French cheese, of course.

Peter : Mm ça semble délicieux ! Je commence à avoir faim. Est-ce qu'on va commander ?

Peter: Mm sounds yummy! I'm starting to get hungry. Shall we order?

Julie: Bien sûr. Qu'est-ce que tu as choisi ?

Julie: Sure. What did you choose?

Peter : Je vais prendre un Coq au vin. Je sais que c'est une spécialité française, mais je n'ai pas encore goûté.

Peter: I'll take a Coq au vin. I know this is a French specialty, but I haven't tried it yet.

Julie : Oui, c'est très bon, moi aussi je vais prendre un.

Julie:
Yes, it is nice, I'll take one too.

……………

…….....

Peter : La prochaine fois on peut aller dans un restaurant italien.

Peter: Next time we can go to an Italian restaurant.

Julie : Pourquoi ? Est-ce que tu t'intéresses à la cuisine italienne ?

Julie: I don't know, maybe. Why? Are you interested in Italian cuisine?

Peter : Oui, en effet. J'ai été en Italie deux fois. La cuisine italienne est délicieuse, et ce n'est pas uniquement de la pizza. Ils ont des desserts fantastiques aussi. Est-ce que tu aimes les sucreries ?

Peter: I am actually. I have been to Italy twice. Italian food is delicious, and it is not only pizza. They have some fantastic desserts too. Do you like sweet things?

Julie :
Oh oui, j'adore !

Julie: Oh yes, very much so! I adore sweet things!

USEFUL VOCABULARY : restaurant, menu, meals

bistrot – pub ; **réserver une table** – book a table

une entrée / des hors-d'œuvre – starter ; **le plat principal** – main course ; **dessert** – dessert

du vin – wine ; **du vin rouge** – red wine ; **blanc** – white ; **sec** – dry ; **doux** – sweet **de la bière** – beer

des boissons non alcoolisées – soft drinks ; **de l'eau minérale** – mineral water**plate** – still ; **gazeuse, pétillante** – sparkling ; **du jus de pomme** – apple juice ; **du jus d'orange** – orange juice

le plat du jour – Today's special

de la viande – meat ; **steak / bleu, saignant** – rare ; **à point** – medium ; **bien cuit** – well-done ; **des pilons de poulet** – chicken drumsticks ; **des ailes de poulet** – chicken winglets ; **des frites** – French fries ; **du riz** – rice ; **du pain à l'ail** – garlic bread

une soupe de poulet – chicken soup ; **une soupe de légumes** – vegetable soup
des œufs pochés – poached eggs ; **des œufs brouillés** – scrambled eggs

du sel – salt ; **du poivre** – pepper ; **des épices** – spices ; **de l'huile d'olive** – olive oil ; **du vinaigre** – vinegar

de la glace – ice cream ; **des biscuits** – cookies ; **un gâteau** – cake

un pourboire – tip

des couverts – cutlery ; **une fourchette** – fork ; **une cuillère** – spoon ; **un couteau** – knife ; **une serviette** – napkin ; **un verre** – glass ; **un verre de vin** – glass of wine
une tasse – cup ; **une tasse de café** – cup of coffee

Useful expressions

Nous n'avons pas réservé. Est-ce que vous avez une table pour quatre personnes? We have not booked (we don't have a reservation). Do you have a table for four?

Désolé, nous ne sommes pas encore prêts à commander. Sorry, we are not ready to order yet.

Vous pouvez nous donner encore quelques minutes, s'il vous plaît ? Could you give us a few more minutes, please?

Nous voudrions commander maintenant, s'il vous plaît. We would like to order now, please.

Je vais prendre… I would like … / I will have …

Est-ce qu'on peut voir la carte des desserts, s'il vous plaît ? Can we see the dessert menu, please?

<u>If you are served something you have not ordered:</u>

Excusez-moi, je n'ai pas commandé ça. Excuse me, I did not order this.

La même chose, s'il vous plaît. Same again, please.

Je peux avoir encore une bière / un verre de vin ? Could I have another beer/ another glass of wine?

C'est délicieux. It is delicious. C'est formidable. It is lovely.

Tout est parfait. Everything is perfect.

<u>Paying the bill :</u>

L'addition, s'il vous plaît ? Could we have the bill, please?

Je peux payer par carte ? Can I pay by credit card?

Gardez la monnaie. Keep the change.

<u>If the bill seems to you too high:</u>

Est-ce que vous pouvez vérifier l'addition, s'il vous plaît ? Je pense qu'il y a une erreur. Could you check the bill for me, please? I think there might be a mistake.

<u>Typical French dishes:</u>

Soupe à l'onion – traditional French soup made of onions and beef stock, usually served with croutons and melted cheese on top.

Coq au vin – chicken braised with wine, mushrooms, salty pork or bacon (lardons), mushrooms, onions, garlic and sometimes even a drop of brandy.

Cassoulet – white beans stewed slowly with meat. The dish typically uses pork or duck but can include sausages, goose or mutton.

Bœuf bourguignon – a stew made from beef braised in red wine, beef broth, and seasoned vegetables including pearl onions and mushrooms.

Confit de canard – fine French dish of duck (sometimes goose or pork). The meat is marinated in salt, garlic, and thyme for hours and then slow-cooked in its own fat at low temperatures. It is typically served with roasted potatoes and garlic on the side

Ratatouille – a variety of vegetables, shallow fried and then baked in the oven.

Chocolat soufflé – light, airy chocolate dessert.

Tarte aux pommes – delicious apple tart, topped off with caramelized apples, fanned in a distinctive spiral pattern.

UNIT 15
IMPARFAIT

Translated by **Past Continuous** (I was working) or **I used to** (work).

Expresses a **past action of undetermined duration** or a repeated action in the past.

HOW
DO WE FORM IT?

> The stem of **1st** person plural (**nous**) au **Présent** + endings:

-ais	-ions
-ais	-iez
-ait	-aient

The endings are the same no matter in which group the verb is, whether it is regular or irregular.

verb I group	verb II group	verb III group
espérer	**réfléchir**	**prendre**
nous **espér**-ons	nous **réfléchiss**-ons	nous **pren**-ons
J'espér**ais**	je réfléchiss**ais**	je pren**ais**
tu espér**ais**	tu réfléchiss**ais**	tu pren**ais**
il/elle espér**ait**	il/elle réfléchiss**ait**	il/elle pren**ait**
nous espér**ions**	nous réfléchiss**ions**	nous pren**ions**
vous espér**iez**	vous réfléchiss**iez**	vous pren**iez**
ils/elles espér**aient**	ils/elles réfléchiss**aient**	ils/elles pren**aient**

<u>avoir</u>

J'avais	nous avions
Tu avais	vous aviez
Il/elle avait	ils/elles avaient

I/you/he…had; was/were having; used to have

Nous avions deux chiens dans le passé. We used to have two dogs.

Ils avaient un appartement en ville, mais ils l'ont vendu. They had an apartment in town but they sold it.

<u>il y a</u>

il y avait – there was / there were

Il y avait suffisamment de place pour tout le monde. There was enough space for everyone.

<u>être</u>

The verb **être** is an exception of the rule. Its forms are not derived from 1st person plural.

j'étais	nous étions
tu étais	vous étiez
il/elle était	ils/elles étaient

I/he/she was; we/you/they were

J'étais timide dans mon enfance. I was shy as a child.

Ils étaient très jeunes quand ils se sont connus. They were very young when they met.

Two impersonal verbs **il faut** and **il pleut**

il faut / must	il fallait / had to
il pleut / it is raining	il pleuvait / it was raining
Il neige / it is snowing	il neigeait / it was snowing

Il pleuvait quand je suis sorti. It was raining when I got out.

Il fallait prendre des mesures. We had to take measures.

(-) Negative form

ne...pas

Je ne travaillais pas, je jouais au tennis avec un ami. I was not working, I was play-ing tennis with a friend of mine.

(?) Question form

est-ce que, intonation, inversion.

Qu'est-ce que tu faisais à 19 heures hier soir ? Je t'ai appelé pour te dire **qu'il y avait** un bon concert à la télé, mais tu n'as pas répondu.

What were you doing yesterday at 7pm? I called you to say there was a nice concert on TV, but you did not answer.

Negative sentences and questions are rare as the tense is descriptive.

WHEN
DO WE USE L'IMPARFAIT?

L'Imparfait usually expresses **continuous actions or situations** in the past and corresponds to Past Continuous in English. It can also express **repeated actions** and in these cases it is translated by "used to".

Je me levais tôt quand j'étais plus jeune. I used to get up early when I was younger.

When *l'Imparfait* describes a continuous action in the past, it is often combined with *Passé composé*. In the middle of a continued action, something else happens.

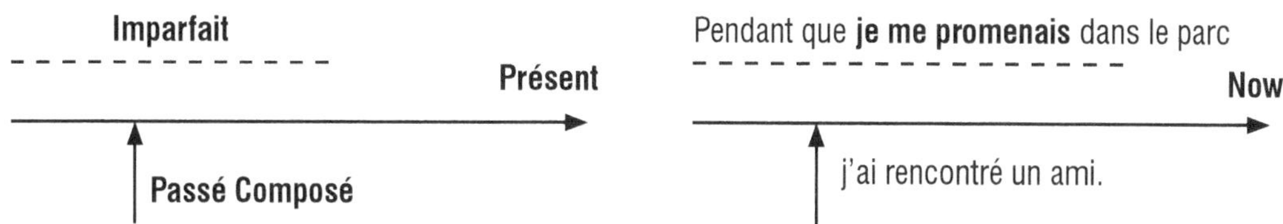

Pendant que **je me promenais** dans le parc, j'ai rencontré un ami.

While I was walking in the park, I met a friend of mine.

se promener – continuous action (Imparfait)

rencontrer l'ami – short action (Passé composé)

Pendant que **je cuisinais**, je me suis blessé.

While I was cooking, I cut myself.

<u>être (Imparfait) en train de + infinitif</u>

This structure is synonym of *Imparfait* when it describes something ongoing in the past.

J'étais en train de travailler. = Je travaillais.

Elle était en train de parler au téléphone. = Elle parlait au téléphone.

Ils étaient en train de discuter. = Ils discutaient.

<u>Key words</u>**:**

> **pendant que** – while
> **quand** – when

Quand is placed before the short action.

Quand elle est arrivée, **nous étions en train de dîner**.
When she arrived, we were having dinner.

Quand il est rentré, **sa femme était en train de cuisiner**.
When he got home, his wife was cooking.

Quand je me suis levé ce matin, **il neigeait**.
When I got up this morning, it was snowing.

Quand il est rentré, **ils étaient en train de** dîner.
When he got home, they were having dinner.

EXERCISES **Conjugate the verbs:**

1. - Ils … (être) en Algérie quand les troubles …. (commencer) They were living in Algeria when the unrest started.

- Est-ce qu'ils … (retourner) en France immédiatement ? Did they come back to France immediately?

- Oui. Yes, they did.

…

2. - Hier matin il … (pleut) si fort que j'… (décider) d'aller au travail en voiture, mais après je …. (regretter). Yesterday morning it was raining so heavily that I decided to go to work by car, but later I regretted it.

- Pourquoi ? Why?

…

- Le trafic …(être) horrible et ça m'a pris deux heures pour aller au travail. The traffic was awful and it took me two hours to get to work.

…

3. - Ce logiciel est très utile. Quand est-ce que tu …(acheter)?

This software is very useful. When did you buy it?

- **En fait, il est gratuit, je … (télécharger).** Pendant que je … (surf) sur Internet l'autre jour je … (voir) une publicité et je … (décider) de l'essayer.

Actually it is free, I downloaded it. While I was surfing on the net the other day I saw an advertisement and decided to give it a try.

…

4. - Désolé que je … (ne pas répondre) au téléphone, mais je… (parler) avec un collègue du Canada. Sorry, I didn't answer your call, I was talking to a collegue of mine from Canada.

- **D'accord, mais pourquoi tu … (ne pas rappeler) plus tard ?**

It's OK. But why didn't you call me back?

- **Parce qu'après je … (être) si occupé que je … (ne pas trouver) de temps.**

Because after that I was so busy that I didn't find time.

…

5. - Au même moment la semaine dernière je … (être) allongé sur la plage et je … (bronzer) au soleil.

This time last week I was lying on the beach and was sunbathing.

- **C'est vrai ? Tu … (être) où ?** Really? Where were you?

- **Je … (être) en vacances en Floride.** I was on holiday in Florida.

DIALOGUE   « Business trip to Barcelona »

Peter is talking to his colleagues about his trip to Barcelona.

Peter : **J'ai failli** rater mon vol pour Barcelone l'autre jour.

Peter: I nearly missed my flight to Barcelona the other day.

Collègue : Pourquoi ? Qu'est-ce qui **s'est passé** ?

Colleague:
Why? What happened?

Peter : **J'étais** sur la route vers l'aéroport quand **je me suis rendu compte** que j'avais oublié la clé avec ma présentation. Du coup, **j'ai dû retourner** à la maison pour la chercher. En plus de ça, le taxi **s'est retrouvé** dans un embouteillage, même si ce n'était pas l'heure de pointe. Quand je suis finalement arrivé à l'aéroport, **on faisait** un dernier appel pour moi. Heureusement, **j'ai réussi** à prendre l'avion et **je suis arrivé** à l'heure pour la conférence.

Peter: I was on my way to the airport when I realized that I had forgotten the flash drive with my presentation. So I had to rush back home to take it. On top of that, the taxi got stuck in a traffic jam, although it was not rush hour. When I finally arrived at the airport, they were making a final call for me. Fortunately, I managed to catch the plane and I was in time for the conference.

Collègue : Est-ce que **tu as eu** le temps de te promener en ville ?

Peter : Oui, et **je l'ai adorée** ! La conférence a fini tard, après 20 heures, et puis nous sommes tous allés nous promener au centre. **Les rues étaient** pleines de monde et **il y avait** tellement de petites boutiques, cafés, restaurants. **On pouvait** entendre la musique venant des bars, **l'ambiance était** fantastique. **On a pris** des tapas dans un petit restaurant, puis on est allés dans un bar. **Tout était** super, seulement j'ai un peu trop bu et **j'avais** la gueule de bois le lendemain !

Colleague: And did you have time to look around the city?

Peter: Yes, I did, and I loved it! The conference finished late, after 8pm, and then we all went for a walk in the centre. The streets were full of people and there were so many little shops, cafes, restaurants. Live music was coming from the bars, the atmosphere was wonderful. We had tapas in a small restaurant, then we went to a bar. Everything was great, except that I got a bit drunk and had a hangover the next morning!

USEFUL VOCABULARY : trips, transport, hôtels, tourism

Transport

voyager – to travel ; **voyage** – journey / trip ; **voyage d'affaires** – business trip **passager** – passenger
en avion – by plane ; **en train** – by train ; **en bus / tram** – by bus / tram
en voiture – by car ; **à vélo** – by bike ; **à pied** – on foot ; **aller à pied** – to walk

Avion – plane

un aéroport – airport ; **un vol** – flight ; **décoller** – take off ; **atterrir** – to land
réserver un vol – to book a flight ; **une réservation** – booking ; **un retard** – delay
un départ – departure ; **un enregistrement (en ligne)** – (online) check in
un bagage à main – hand luggage ; **une porte** – gate ; **un embarquement** – boarding ; **une carte d'embarquement** – boarding pass ; **une ceinture de protection** – seat belt ; **un équipage** – crew ; **une hôtesse de l'air, un steward** – flight attendant ; **une arrivée** – arrival ; **une livraison des bagages** – baggage (re)claim
le contrôle à la frontière – border control ; **une carte d'identité** – identity card ; **la nationalité** – nationality ; **le but du voyage** – purpose of the trip
un séjour – stay ; **un pays de résidence** – country of residence ; **une visite privée** – private visit ; **un voyage d'affaires** – business trip ; **la douane** – customs ; **rien à declarer** – nothing to declare ; **un douanier** – customs officer
zone hors taxe – duty free zone ; **c'est permis** – it's allowed ; **c'est interdit** – it's forbidden

Bus – bus

prendre le bus – to catch the bus ; **monter** – to get on ; **descendre** – to get off
un arrêt de bus – bus stop ; **une station** – bus station

Train – train

prendre le train – to catch a train ; **les horaires** – timetable ; **un billet aller retour** – return ticket ; **la première / seconde classe** – first/second class **une gare** – railway station ; **un quai** – platform ; **une voiture, un wagon** – carriage

Voiture – car

une route – road ; **sur la route** – on the road ; **une autoroute** – motorway/highway ; **un permis de conduire** – driving licence ; **une place de stationnement** – parking lot ; **conduire** – to drive ; **tourner** – to turn ; **tomber en panne** – to break down ; **réparer** – to repair/fix ; **un réservoir** – tank ; **un siège** – seat **une ceinture** – safety belt ; **un pneu** – tyre ; **un pneu à plat** – flat tyre **un moteur** – engine ; **la malle** – boot ; **des pièces détachées** – spare parts **faire du stop** – to go hitchhiking

Hôtel – hotel

une réservation – booking/reservation ; **un séjour** – stay ; **une chambre double** – double room ; **une chambre individuelle** – single room **un appartement** – suite ; **un climatiseur** – air-conditioner ; **petit déjeuner compris** – breakfast included ; **chambre et petit déjeuner** – bed and breakfast
une grande ville – city ; **la capitale** – capital ; **une petite ville** – town **un village** – village ; **à la campagne** – in the countryside ; **la montagne** – mountain ; **la mer** – sea ; **aller à la mer** – to go to the seaside ; **un océan** – ocean **une rivière** – river ; **un lac** – lake

Ville – city

L'Hôtel de ville – City hall ; **la Gare** – Station ; **la Poste** – Post office **une école** – school ; **une université** – University ; **un musée** – museum **un théâtre** – theatre ; **une banque** – bank ; **une église** – church **une mosquée** – mosque ; **un hôpital** – hospital ; **la vieille ville** – Old town **le centre ville** – city centre / downtown ; **un port** – port/harbour **une banlieue** – suburb ; **un quartier résidentiel** – residential district **un quartier, un voisinage** – neighbourhood ; **une rue** – street ; **un boulevard** – avenue ; **une place** – square ; **le périphérique** – ring-road ; **un carrefour** – crossroads ; **les feux** – traffic lights ; **un trottoir** – footpath / sidewalk

Magasins – Shops

un supermarché – supermarket ; **un centre commercial** – department store / mall **une boulangerie** – baker's ; **une boucherie** – butcher's ; **une épicerie** – grocery shop ; **fruits et légumes** – greengrocer's ; **un fleuriste** – florist's **une librairie** – bookshop ; **une bijouterie** – jewellery shop

UNIT 16

PLUS-QUE-PARFAIT

Translated in English by **Past Perfect** (I had worked) or **Past Perfect Continuous** (I had been working)

HOW
DO WE FORM IT ?

It is similar to *Passé composé*, but the auxiliary verb **avoir** (or **être**) is conjugated in **Imparfait**.

> **avoir** (or être) à l'Imparfait + **participe passé**

avoir à l'Imparfait

J'avais	nous avions
Tu avais	vous aviez
Il/elle avait	ils/elles avaient

Example : Plus-que-parfait of the verb **parler**

J'avais parlé	nous avions parlé
Tu avais parlé	vous aviez parlé
Il/elle avait parlé	ils/elles avaient parlé

Il avait parlé avec le chef avant de prendre cette décision. He had talked to the boss before making this decision.

être à l'Imparfait

j'étais	nous étions
tu étais	vous étiez
il/elle était	ils/elles étaient

The verbs conjugated with **être** in **Passé composé** are also conjugated with **être** in **Plus-que-parfait**.

Example : Plus-que-parfait of the verb **arriver**

j'étais arrivé(e)	nous étions arrivé(e)s
tu étais arrivé(e)	vous étiez arrivé(e)s
Il était arrivé Elle était arrivée	ils étaient arrivés elles étaient arrivées

Ils étaient arrivés plus tôt que prévu. They had arrived earlier than expected.

All the rules of the formation of *Passé composé* are valid here: most verbs take the auxiliary **avoir**, and a small group of verbs plus the pronominal (reflexive) verbs take **être**. (see Unit 14)

Negative form

ne...pas

Je n'avais pas pris de parapluie. I had not taken an umbrella.

Question form

est-ce que, intonation, inversion

Est-ce que tu avais dit à ton manager ? Had you told your manager?

WHEN
DO WE USE PLUS-QUE-PARFAIT?

We use it to talk about an action which occurred **before another past action.** This past action is expressed by *Passé composé*.

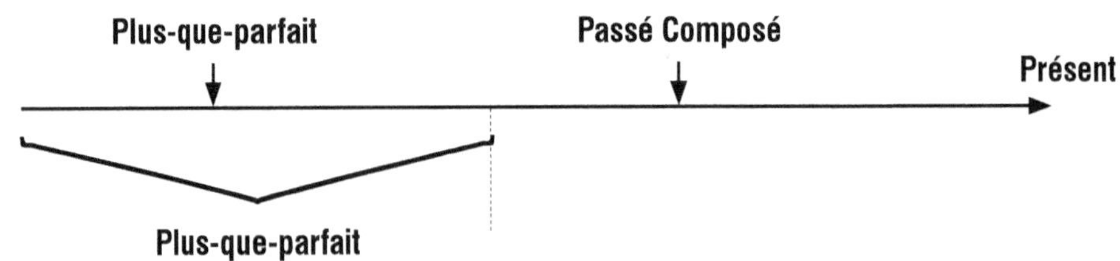

- <u>Short action</u>, occurred before a past moment

(translated by Past Perfect)

Je ne suis pas allé au cinéma avec mes amis, parce que **j'avais déjà vu** ce film.
I did not go to the cinema with my friends because I had already seen this film.

Quand je suis arrivé au stade, **le match avait déjà commencé**.
By the time I got to the stadium, the match had already started.

- <u>Continuous action</u>

(translated by Past Perfect Continuous):

Il avait mal à la tête. **Il avait travaillé** sur l'ordinateur toute la journée.

He had a headache. He had been working on the computer all day.

Quand il est arrivé, **le bus était déjà parti**.
When he arrived the bus had just left.

Nous avions joué pendant un moment quand il a commencé à pleuvoir.
We had been playing for a while when it started to rain.

Le *Passé récent* (**venir de + infinitif**) can also be related to a past moment and then **venir** is conjugated in *Imparfait* (je venais de…, tu venais de…)

Je n'avais pas faim. **Je venais de déjeuner.** I was not hungry. I had just had lunch.

DIALOGUE   « Injury during a tennis match »

Peter and Olivier played tennis last Sunday. During the game Peter got injured and had to go to the doctor. The next day he is talking to Julie about this:

Julie : Pourquoi tu boites ? Qu'est-ce que tu as à la jambe ?

Peter : Hier après-midi je suis allé jouer au tennis avec mon ami Olivier. **Il avait plu** et le court était un peu glissant. Mais, moi **j'avais parié** 20 livres que j'allais gagner, donc il n'était pas question d'annuler le jeu. Tout allait bien, j'ai gagné le premier set et je menais dans le deuxième quand j'ai glissé, je suis tombé et je me suis tordu la cheville.

Julie : Le pauvre, tu as perdu 20 livres !

Peter : Très drôle ! ☹ En fait j'avais si mal que j'ai dû aller chez le médecin. J'ai dû faire une radio. Heureusement pas de fracture, mais je ne pourrai pas jouer au tennis pendant un certain temps.

Julie : Tu vas te remettre vite.

Peter : J'espère. Mais d'ici-là je dois rester à la maison la plupart du temps. Tu ne veux pas venir dimanche ? Je peux te cuisiner quelque chose de spécial.

Julie : Hmm, tu m'avais promis de m'amener à un restaurant italien, tu ne te rappelles pas ?

Peter : Bien sûr que je me rappelle. On va y aller aussitôt que je serai remis. Maintenant je t'invite chez moi à goûter les spécialités françaises que j'ai appris à faire. Je suis très bon en cuisine ☺

Julie : Des spécialités françaises ? On verra ça...

Julie: Why are you limping? What's wrong with your leg?

Peter: Yesterday afternoon I went to play tennis with my friend Olivier. It had been raining and the court was a bit slippery. But I had bet 20 pounds that I would win so there was no way to cancel the game. Everything was going well, I won the first set and I was leading in the second when I slipped, fell down and sprained my ankle.

Julie: Poor you, you lost 20 pounds!

Peter: Very funny! ☹ In fact it hurt so much that I had to go to the doctor. I had to get an X ray. Fortunately it is not broken, but I won't be able to play tennis for a while.

Julie: You'll be OK soon.

Peter: I hope so. But until then I must stay at home most of the time. Why don't you come to my place on Sunday? I will cook you something special.

Julie: Hmm you had promised to take me to an Italian restaurant, don't you remember?

Peter: Of course I do, we'll go as soon as I get better. Now I invite you to try the French dishes that I have learnt to cook. I am very good at cooking ☺

Julie: French dishes? We'll see...

USEFUL VOCABULARY : body, health

Corps – Body

la tête – head ; **le visage** – face ; **le front** – forehead ; **la peau** – skin ; **les cheveux** – hair ; **les yeux** – eyes ; **les sourcils** – eyebrows ; **les cils** – eyelashes
les oreilles – ears ; **le nez** – nose ; **la bouche** – mouth ; **la dent** – tooth ; **la langue** – tongue ; **les gencives** – gums ; **une lèvre** – lip ; **une joue** – cheek ; **le menton** – chin
le cou – neck ; **la gorge** – throat ; **les épaules** – shoulders ; **la poitrine** – chest
les seins – breasts ; **le bras** – arm ; **le coude** – elbow ; **la main** – hand ; **le poignet** – wrist ; **les doigts** – fingers ; **les ongles** – nails ; **le dos** – back ; **la taille** – waist
la hanche – hip ; **la cuisse** – thigh ; **la jambe** – leg ; **le genou** – knee ; **le pied** – foot **la cheville** – ankle ; **le talon** – heel ; **un orteil** – toe

le cœur – heart ; **le cerveau** – brain ; **le sang** – blood ; **les poumons** – lungs
 un estomac – stomach ; **le foie** – liver ; **les reins** – kidneys

les sens – senses

l'ouïe – hearing ; **la vue** – eyesight ; **l'odorat** – sense of smell ; **le sens du toucher** – sense of touch ; **le goût** – taste

entendre – to hear ; **écouter** – to listen ; **voir** – to see ; **regarder** – to look, to watch
sentir – to smell ; **une odeur** – smell ; **un parfum** – scent ; **toucher** – to touch
goûter – to taste

la santé – health ; **en bonne santé, sain** – healthy ; **un mode de vie sain** – healthy life style

être malade – to be sick / to be ill ; **tomber malade** – to get sick ; **prendre froid** – to catch a cold ; **avoir la grippe** – to have the flu

tousser – to cough ; **être enrhumé** – to have a runny nose ; **éternuer** – to sneeze
avoir mal à la gorge – to have a sore throat ; **avoir la fièvre** – to have a fever
avoir mal à la tête – to have a headache ; **avoir le vertige** – to feel dizzy

une douleur – ache/pain ; **avoir mal à la dent** – to have a toothache ; **avoir mal** – it hurts

un médicament – medicine / drug ; **une pilule / un comprimé** – pill / tablet
une ordonnance – prescription ; **sans ordonnance** – over-the-counter

J'ai mal au dos. My back hurts.

Est-ce que vous avez mal ? Does it hurt?

Où est-ce que vous avez mal ? Where does it hurt?

Remets-toi vite ! Get well soon!

Je me remets. I am getting better.

PAST TENSES – summary

Passé composé, Imparfait, Plus-que-parfait

1. Passé composé + Imparfait

**Quand je me suis levé,
elle était en train de faire des
crêpes.**

When I got up,
she was making pancakes.

2. Passé composé + Plus-que-parfait

**Quand je me suis levé,
elle avait fait des crêpes.**

When I got up,
she had made some pancakes.

3. Passé composé + Passé composé

**Quand je me suis levé,
nous avons fait des crêpes.**

When I got up,
we made some pancakes.

Example – a weekend from real life:

Last weekend, we decided to go to the mountain with the children to escape from the great heat. We called some friends of ours to ask if they wanted to come with us. We went together and while the children were playing, we were sitting and talking about different things – football, tennis, music. I had not seen the Wimbledon final and my friends told me what had happened.

Le weekend dernier, pour fuir la canicule, **on a décidé** d'aller à la montagne avec les enfants. **On a appelé** des amis pour leur proposer de venir avec nous, **s'ils aimaient** l'idée. Alors **nous sommes allés** ensemble, et pendant que **les enfants jouaient**, **nous discutions** des sujets divers – du football, du tennis, de la musique. **Je n'avais pas vu** la finale de tennis à Wimbledon, et **mes amis m'ont raconté** ce qui **s'était passé.**

Past tenses here:

Passé composé – **4** times:

on a décidé ; On a appelé ; nous sommes allés ; mes amis m'ont raconté

Imparfait – **3** times:

s'ils aimaient ; les enfants jouaient ; nous discutions

Plus-que-parfait – **twice:**

Je n'avais pas vu ; ce qui **s'était passé.**

   Conjugate the verbs:

Il y a quelques jours nous …. (avoir) un problème désagréable dans notre immeuble. Les techniciens qui … (faire) des travaux dans l'appartement au deuxième étage, … (obstruer) une conduite d'eau dans la salle de bains. Dimanche un voisin … (découvrir) par hasard que … (il y a) une inondation dans la cave. En fait, nous … (ne pas comprendre) quand ça … (commencer). On … (devoir) appeler une équipe technique d'urgence, et la visite… (être) beaucoup plus chère que durant la semaine. En plus de tout, pendant qu'ils … (travailler), leur machine … (tomber) en panne, et ils … (ne pas pouvoir) régler le problème. Le lendemain ils … (revenir) pour terminer le travail, mais aussitôt ils … (se rendre compte) qu'ils … (oublier) une pièce nécessaire pour remplacer la conduite. Ils … (devoir) arrêter et aller l'acheter, ce qui … (prendre) pas mal de temps. Avant qu'ils aient finalement terminé nous … (rester) sans douche pendant deux journées entières !

A few days ago we had an annoying problem in our building. The handymen who were renovating the apartment on the second floor blocked a water pipe in the bathroom. On Sunday one neighbour discovered by accident that there was a flooding in the basement. We actually did not understand when exactly it had started. We had to call an emergency technician group and the visit was much more expensive than on a working day. On top of that, while they were working, their machine broke down and they could not fix the problem. The next day they came back to continue but they soon realized that they had forgotten a part which was necessary to replace the pipe. So they had to stop and go to buy it, which took quite a long time. By the time they completed the job, we had been without a shower for two days!

The use of verb tenses can be compared to a tool box. You know what instrument you need in every situation – if you are talking about habits, things in general, or about what you are doing at the moment or your future plans and arrangements – *le Présent* ; if you are telling a friend about your holiday or past weekend – *Passé composé, Imparfait, Plus-que-parfait*.

When we talk about the future, we can choose among several options which we will see in the next unit.

UNIT 17

FUTUR

There are <u>three</u> future tenses in French:

le Futur proche, le Futur simple, le Futur antérieur

Le **Futur proche** is the most commonly used future tense in everyday conversations and it is the easiest to form.

FUTUR PROCHE

Translated by **be going to + infinitive** (I am going to work) or Future Simple (I will work)

HOW do we form it ?

aller + infinitif

Aller is an auxiliary verb here, and does not mean « go »

je vais	nous allons
tu vas	vous allez
il/elle va	ils/elles vont

Je vais vérifier. I will check.

Il va acheter du pain. He is going to buy some bread.

Ils vont m'aider. They are going to help me.

On va voir. We'll see.

(-) <u>**Negative form**</u>

ne...pas

Je ne vais pas faire un gâteau. I'm not going to make a cake.

Je ne pense pas qu'elle va m'appeler. I don't think she is going to call me.

(?) <u>**Question form**</u>

est-ce que, **intonation**, **inversion**

Est-ce que tu vas aller à cette réunion ? Are you going to this meeting?

Est-ce qu'il va te prêter de l'argent ? Is he going to lend you some money?

(- ?) <u>**Negative question**</u>

Est-ce que tu ne vas pas réserver une table ? Aren't you going to book a table?

Est-ce qu'il ne va pas postuler pour ce travail ? Isn't he going to apply for this job?

<u>WHEN</u>
<u>DO WE USE LE FUTUR PROCHE ?</u>

- When we talk about an action that will take place <u>shortly</u>.

Je vais prendre le parapluie. I'll take the umbrella.

Il va pleuvoir cet après-midi. It is going to rain this afternoon.

- When we talk about a <u>planned action in the near future</u>.

On va acheter une petite table pour le salon. We are going to buy a small table for the living room.

L'entreprise va faire une réorganisation. The company is going to reorganize.

FUTUR SIMPLE

HOW do we form it ?

> **Infinitif du verbe + terminaisons**

-ai	-ons
-as	-ez
-a	-ont

verb I group		verb II group	
parler		**choisir**	
Je parler**ai**	nous parler**ons**	je choisir**ai**	nous choisir**ons**
Tu parler**as**	vous parler**ez**	tu choisir**as**	vous choisir**ez**
Il/elle parler**a**	ils/elles parler**ont**	il/elle choisir**a**	ils/elles choisir**ont**

Verbs III group

- Most verbs ending in **-ir**, like **ouvrir** and **sortir** are regular. You add the endings to the infinitive. Exceptions: courir, mourir (je courrai, je mourrai)

- With the verbs which end in **-re**, the final « e » is dropped and replaced by the endings:

dire		**mettre**	
Je dir**ai**	nous dir**ons**	je mettr**ai**	nous mettr**ons**
Tu dir**as**	vous dir**ez**	tu mettr**as**	vous mettr**ez**
Il/elle dir**a**	ils/elles dir**ont**	il/elle mettr**a**	ils/elles mettr**ont**

Similar: boire, connaître, construire, croire, écrire, lire, plaire, prendre, vendre, vivre.

Irregular verbs

être		**avoir**	
Je serai	**nous serons**	**J'aurai**	**nous aurons**
Tu seras	**vous serez**	**Tu auras**	**vous aurez**
Il/elle sera	**ils/elles seront**	**il/elle aura**	**ils/elles auront**

aller		faire	
J'irai	nous irons	Je ferai	nous ferons
Tu iras	vous irez	Tu feras	vous ferez
Il/elle ira	ils/elles iront	il/elle fera	ils/elles feront

devoir		pouvoir	
Je devrai	nous devrons	Je pourrai	nous pourrons
Tu devras	vous devrez	Tu pourras	Vous pourrez
Il/elle devra	ils/elles devront	il/elle pourra	ils/elles pourront

recevoir		savoir	
Je recevrai	nous recevrons	Je saurai	nous saurons
Tu recevras	vous recevrez	Tu sauras	vous saurez
Il/elle recevra	ils/elles recevront	il/elle saura	ils/elles sauront

venir		voir	
Je viendrai	nous viendrons	Je verrai	nous verrons
Tu viendras	vous viendrez	Tu verras	vous verrez
Il/elle viendra	ils/elles viendront	il/elle verra	ils/elles verront

vouloir	
Je voudrai	nous voudrons
Tu voudras	vous voudrez
Il/elle voudra	ils/elles voudront

Some verbs have a little different spelling in **Futur simple**: **peser** – je pèserai (the first « e » gets **accent grave**); **jeter** – je jetterai (« t » is doubled); **appeler** – j'appellerai (« l » is doubled).

<u>WHEN</u>
<u>DO WE USE LE FUTUR SIMPLE?</u>

<u>1. Far Future</u>
Un jour **je saurai** pourquoi il a fait ça. One day I will know why he did it.

Dans 30 ans **on aura** beaucoup de sources d'énergie écologique. In some 30 years time, we will have a lot of clean energy sources.

<u>2. Forecast</u>
Je pense que **tu auras** suffisamment de temps. I think you will have enough time.

<u>3. In Conditional sentences</u>
Si tu révises bien, **tu réussiras** ton examen. If you work hard, you will pass the test.

S'il fait beau ce weekend, **on ira** à la plage. If the weather is nice this weekend, we will go to the beach.

<u>Note</u> : **Le Future proche** is also possible: tu réussiras / tu vas réussir ; on ira / on va aller.

<u>4. Asking politely</u>
Vous demanderez à Mme Laforce de venir dans mon bureau, s'il vous plaît?
Would you ask Mme Laforce to come to my office, please?

5. With <u>**dès que, lorsque, quand**</u>
Dès que tu arriveras, appelle-moi !

Quand je reviendrai en France, on fera une réunion des vieux camarades de classe. When I come back to France, we will hold a class reunion.

Note : We can also use **le Présent** in these cases:
dès que tu arriveras/dès que tu arrives ; quand je reviendrai / quand je reviens.

Le Futur simple is more formal, more classic, and less commonly used in spoken French than le **Futur proche**.

Having said that, we must note that some verbs are more often used in **Futur simple** than in **Futur proche**, even in a common converstaion, like for example, **être, avoir, devoir, pouvoir**.

Je serai très occupé la semaine prochaine. I am going to be very busy next week.

Nous n'aurons pas le droit de remboursement. We won't have the right to a refund.

Je devrai parler avec mon manager. I will have to talk with my manager.

On ne pourra pas arriver a temps. We won't be able to arrive on time.

Some common expressions are said both ways:

> **On va voir.** = **On verra.** We'll see.
> **Ça va aller.** = **Ça ira.** It will be OK.

<u>ETRE (Futur) + en train de...</u>

It Corresponds to Future Continuous (I will be doing) and expresses an activity which will be in progress in the future.

Je serai en train de travailler. I will be working.

En ce moment la semaine prochaine **je serai en train de bronzer** sur la plage.
This time next week I will be sunbathing on the beach.

Ne l'appelle pas ce soir! **Il sera en train de regarder** la finale, et tu sais comment il est passionné.
Don't call him tonight! He will be watching the final, and you know what a crazy fan he is.

We can make a comparison between:

J'étais en train de... / Imparfait (*Past Continuous*).

Je suis en train de.../ le Present (*Present Continuous*)

Je serai en train de...(*Future Continuous*).

The three options express a continuing activity. The choice depends on <u>**when**</u> the activity is happening – in the past, in the present or in the future:

Hier soir à 21 heures **j'étais en train de regarder** la télé.	At 9 pm last night I was watching TV.
Il est 21 heures, **je suis en train de regarder** la télé.	It is 9 pm now, I am watching TV.
Demain soir à 21 heures, **je serai en train de regarder** la télé.	At 9 pm tomorrow night I will be watching TV.

FUTUR ANTERIEUR

Translated by Future Perfect (I will have done) or Future Perfect Continuous (I will have been doing)

HOW do we form it ?

> **avoir / être (Futur) + participe passé**

Example:

prendre

J'aurai pris	nous aurons pris
Tu auras pris	vous aurez pris
Il/elle aura pris	ils/elles auront pris

Those verbs which are conjugated with **être** in **Passé composé** and in **Plus-que-parfait**, are also conjugated with **être** in **Futur antérieur**.

arriver

Je serai arrivé(e)	nous serons arrivé(e)s
Tu seras arrivé(e)	vous serez arrivé(e)s
Il sera arrivé / elle sera arrivée	ils seront arrivés / elles seront arrivées

The negative form is made with **ne...pas**, and the question – with **est-ce que, intonation, inversion**.

WHEN
DO WE USE LE FUTUR ANTÉRIEUR?

When we talk about an action which will be completed before some point of time in the future.

Le film aura fini avant 23 heures. The film will have finished by 11 pm.

Ils seront arrivés avant la fin de la semaine. They will have arrived by the end of the week.

Vers la fin de l'année **elle aura travaillé** pour cette entreprise pendant 20 ans. By the end of the year she will have been working for this company for 20 years.

EXERCISES   Conjugate the verbs:

1. - Je … (faire) quelque chose pour le dîner. Tu as faim ? I am going to make something for dinner. Are you hungry?

- Pas vraiment. Je … (prendre) une bière d'abord.

Not really. I'll have a beer first.

…

2. – Nous … (aller) à Disneyland le mois prochain. We are going to Disneyland next month.

- Super ! Les enfants … (adorer) ! Great! The children will love it.

…

3. - Tu sais que Eva … (avoir) une promotion ? Did you hear that Eva is going to get a promotion.

- C'est vrai ? Et bien, elle le mérite ! Je … (appeler) tout à l'heure pour la féliciter. Really? Well, she deserves it! I'll call her later to congratulate her.

…

4. - Qu'est-ce que tu … (faire) ce soir ? What are you doing tonight?

- Il y a un match à la télé, je …. (probablement le regarder). There is a football match on the TV, I'll probably watch it.

- A quelle heure il …(commencer) ? What time does it start?

- A 20 heures 45, comme d'habitude. At 8.45 as usual.

…

5. - Est-ce que tu penses que Dany and Eve … (arriver) avant que je sois rentré ? Do you think Eve and Dany will have arrived by the time I get home?

- Je ne sais pas. Je … (les appeler) pour demander à quelle heure … (arriver) leur bus. I don't know. I'll call them to ask what time their bus arrives.

…

6. Je … (nettoyer). I am going to clean.

- Tu peux attendre un peu ? Quand je … (finir) mon jeu, je … (t'aider).

Can you hold on for a little while, please? When I finish this game I will help you.

- **Un peu ? Tu plaisantes ! Avant que tu finisses ton jeu, je … (nettoyer) toute la maison.** A little while? You must be joking! By the time you finish your game, I will have cleaned the whole house.

…

7. - Vers la fin d'avril, on … (habiter) ici pendant 10 ans. By the end of April we will have lived here for 10 years.

- **Pour moi c'est comme si c'était hier qu'on a acheté la maison.** It seems to me as if it was yesterday when we bought the house.

DIALOGUE « A concert in Paris »

Peter is talking to Julie during the lunch break.

Peter : Tu sais que ma sœur Kate vient dans quelques jours. **Elle va rester** deux semaines.

Peter: You know, my sister Kate is coming in a few days. She is going to stay for two weeks.

Julie : C'est super ! **Tu auras** assez de temps pour lui montrer les endroits les plus intéressants. Est-ce qu'elle a déjà été en France ?

Julie: That's great! You will have enough time to show her the most interesting places. Has she been to France before?

Peter : Non, jamais. Elle est très curieuse et m'a dit de lui faire un programme, mais ce n'est pas facile. Nous avons des intérêts complètement différents, et en plus tu sais que maintenant je ne peux pas marcher beaucoup à cause de ma jambe blessée.

Peter: No, she hasn't. She is very curious and told me to make a programme for her, but it is not so easy. We have completely different interests, plus you know that I cannot walk a lot because of my injured leg.

Julie : Je pourrais t'aider. Est-ce qu'elle est plus jeune ou plus âgée que toi ?

Julie: I may be able to help you. Is she younger or older than you?

Peter : Elle est plus jeune. Elle est en quatrième année à l'université.

Peter: She is younger. She is fourth year at university.

Julie : Elle s'intéresse à la musique ?

Julie: Is she interested in music?

Peter : Absolument ! Elle est tout le temps sur Spotify.

Peter: Absolutely! She is on Spotify all the time.

Julie : Alors j'ai une idée. **Je vais** au concert d'Adèle et je propose qu'elle vienne avec moi. Un de mes amis connaît bien les sponsors et peut trouver d'autres billets. Y compris pour toi, si tu veux, mais je ne pense pas que tu sois fan d'Adèle.

Julie: Then I have an idea. I am going to Adele's concert and I suggest taking her with me. A friend of mine is close to the sponsors and can find some more tickets. For you too, if you want to come, but I don't think you are a fan of Adele.

Peter : Pas vraiment, tu sais que je suis fan de hard rock. Mais je suis sûr que **ma sœur sera** aux anges. Merci beaucoup pour l'idée ! Après le concert je vais vous inviter toutes les deux à dîner chez moi.

Peter: Not really, you know I am a hard rock fan. But I'm sure that my sister will be in heaven. Thank you so much for the idea! After the concert I will invite you both home for dinner.

Julie :
Tu vas préparer les fameuses spécialités dont tu m'as déjà parlé ?

Julie: Are you going to cook those special delicious things you have been talking to me about?

Peter : Oui, c'est ça.

Peter: Yes, exactly.

USEFUL VOCABULARY: éducation, work, professions

<u>**Education**</u>

Crèche – crèche ; **une école maternelle** – kindergarten ; **une école primaire** – primary school ; **un collège, un lycée** – secondary school ; **une fac** – college **des études supérieures** – higher education ; **un certificat, un diplôme** – certificate **l'obtention de son diplôme** – graduation ; **une licence** – bachelor's degree **un master** – master's degree ; **un doctorat, un docteur** – PhD (Ph D is contracted of « Doctor of Philosophy ». All sciences are originated from philosophy.) ; **une science** – science ; **un scientifique** – scientist

l'économie – economics ; **le droit** – law ; **la médecine** – medicine ; **la philologie** – philology; **la philosophie** – philosophy ; **la psychologie** – psychology ; **la physique** – physics ; **la biologie** – biology ; **la chimie** – chemistry ; **la génie civil** – civil engineering ; **l'architecture** – architecture

Work

avoir un emploi – have a job ; **postuler** – apply for a job

Qu'est-ce que tu fais dans la vie ? What do you do ? / What is your job?

Où est-ce que tu travailles ? Where do you work?

Depuis quand tu travailles pour cette entreprise ? How long have you been working for this company?

Est-ce que tu aimes ton travail ? Do you like your job?

J'aime mon travail, même s'il est un peu stressant parfois. I like my job although it is a bit stressful sometimes.

Tu vas souvent en voyage d'affaires ? Do you often go on a business trip?

être au chômage – be unemployed

renvoyer – fire ; **quitter** – quit ; **un préavis** – notice

Professions

un ingénieur – engineer ; **un architecte** – architect ; **un comptable** – accountant **un économiste** – economist ; **un(e) enseignant(e)** – teacher ; **un interprète** – interpreter ; **un/une journaliste** – journalist ; **un avocat** – lawyer ; **un juge** – judge

un pharmacien, un chimiste – chemist ; **un médecin** – doctor ; **un vétérinaire** – vet ; **un/une dentiste** – dentist ; **une infirmière** – nurse ; **une sage-femme** – midwife

un acteur – actor ; **une actrice** – actress ; **un chanteur / une chanteuse** – singer **un danseur/une danseuse** – dancer ; **un musicien/une musicienne** – musician **un peintre** – painter ; **un écrivain** – writer ; **un entraîneur** – sport coach

un chef cuisinier – chef ; **un couturier/une couturière** – dressmaker ; **un coiffeur/une coiffeuse** – hairdresser ; **un facteur** – postman ; **un réceptionniste** – receptionist **un responsable administratif** – office manager

un conducteur, un chauffeur – driver ; **un technicien** – mechanic / technician **un serveur/une serveuse** – waiter ; **un vendeur/une vendeuse** – shop assistant ; **un ouvrier/une ouvrière** – worker ; **un charpentier/un menuisier** – carpenter **un plombier** – plumber ; **un électricien** – electrician ; **un pompier** – fireman **un policier** – policeman ; **un pilote** – pilot ; **un steward/une hôtesse de l'air** – flight attendant

Economics

une entreprise/une société – company; **un entrepreneur** – entrepreneur
un directeur/une directrice/un responsable – manager ; **un/une propriétaire** –
owner ; **un personnel** – staff ; **un service/un département** – department
une branche/une agence – branch ; **un client/une cliente** – customer / client
un marché – market ; **le libre marché** – free market ; **investir / un investissement** –
invest / investment ; **un commerce / un commerçant** – trade / trader ; **la bourse** –
stock exchange ; **des actions** – shares ; **un actionnaire** – shareholder ; **le prix du
marché** – market price ; **une liste des prix** – price list ; **fournir** – to supply ; **livrer
/ une livraison** – to deliver / delivery ; **un courrier** – courier

faire la publicité – to advertize ; **une publicité** – advertisement ; **une réduction** –
discount ; **un reçu** – receipt ; **une facture** – invoice ; **un bénéfice** – profit ; **un achat** –
purchase ; **une bonne affaire/ négocier** – bargain ; **un chiffre d'affaires** – turnover
un revenu – income ; **des dépenses** – expenses ; **une taxe/des impôts** – tax **une
amende** – fine

CHAPITRE 18

CONDITIONNEL

Conditionnel présent and Conditionnel passé

You can find these two verb tenses in conditional («if») sentences which are used, as in English, in the following situations:

REALISTIC CONDITION IN THE FUTURE

Si j'ai ..., je ferai...

If I have..., I will do...

We use this structure to talk about something which is likely to happen in the future under a certain condition.

Si + Présent   ..., ...   **Futur simple** or **Futur proche**

First part of the sentence   Second part of the sentence

Si j'ai du temps demain, **je vais faire** les courses.
If I have time tomorrow, I will do the shopping.

S'il ne pleut pas dimanche, **nous allons jouer** au tennis.
If it does not rain on Sunday, we will play tennis.

Si je finis le travail avant 18 heures, **j'irai** au cinéma avec ma copine.
If I finish work before 6pm, I will go to the cinema with my girlfriend.

S'il y a une longue queue, **je ne vais pas attendre**.
If there is a long queue, I will not wait.

« Je peux faire » (I might do) can be used instead of « je vais faire » (I will do).

S'il fait beau ce weekend, **je peux aller** à la montagne. (this is an option)

If the weather is nice this weekend, I might go to the mountain.

Si tu veux / Si vous voulez – If you like

IMAGINARY SITUATION

Si j'avais ..., je ferais

If I had..., I would do...

Si + Imparfait	**... , ...**	**Conditionnel présent**
First part of the sentence		Second part of the sentence

Conditionnel présent

HOW
DO WE FORM IT ?

Le **Conditionnel présent** is very similar to **Futur simple**, because it is formed from the infinitive, but the endings we add are different – they are the typical endings for **Imparfait**:

-ais	**-ions**
-ais	**-iez**
-ait	**-aient**

verb I group		verb II group	
parler		**choisir**	
Je parler**ais**	nous parler**ions**	je choisir**ais**	nous choisir**ions**
Tu parler**ais**	vous parler**iez**	tu choisir**ais**	vous choisir**iez**
Il/elle parler**ait**	ils/elles parler**aient**	il/elle choisir**ait**	ils/elles choisir**aient**

Verbs III group

- Most verbs ending in **-ir**, like **ouvrir** and **sortir** are regular. You add the endings to the infinitive. Exceptions : courir, mourir (je courrais, je mourrais)

- With the verbs which end in **-re**, the final « e » is dropped and replaced by the endings:

dire		mettre	
Je dir**ais**	nous dir**ions**	je mettr**ais**	nous mettr**ions**
Tu dir**ais**	vous dir**iez**	tu mettr**ais**	vous mettr**iez**
Il/elle dir**ait**	ils/elles dir**aient**	il/elle mettr**ait**	ils/elles mettr**aient**

Similar : **boire, connaître, construire, croire, écrire, lire, plaire, prendre, vendre, vivre.**

Irregular verbs

être		avoir	
Je serais	**nous serions**	**J'aurais**	**nous aurions**
Tu serais	**vous seriez**	**Tu aurais**	**vous auriez**
Il/elle serait	**ils/elles seraient**	**il/elle aurait**	**ils/elles auraient**

aller		faire	
J'irais	nous irions	Je ferais	nous ferions
Tu irais	vous iriez	Tu ferais	vous feriez
Il/elle irait	ils/elles iraient	il/elle ferait	ils/elles feraient

devoir		pouvoir	
Je devrais	nous devrions	Je pourrais	nous pourrions
Tu devrais	vous devriez	Tu pourrais	Vous pourriez
Il/elle devrait	ils/elles devraient	il/elle pourrait	ils/elles pourraient

recevoir		savoir	
Je recevrais	nous recevrions	Je saurais	nous saurions
Tu recevrais	vous recevriez	Tu saurais	vous sauriez
Il/elle recevrait	ils/elles recevraient	il/elle saurait	ils/elles sauraient

venir		voir	
Je viendrais	nous viendrions	Je verrais	nous verrions
Tu viendrais	vous viendriez	Tu verrais	vous verriez
Il/elle viendrait	ils/elles viendraient	il/elle verrait	ils/elles verraient

vouloir	
Je voudrais	nous voudrions
Tu voudrais	vous voudriez
Il/elle voudrait	ils/elles voudraient

WHEN do we use it ?

1. <u>Imaginary situation</u>, different from reality. We are talking about something which would happen under some condition.

Si j'avais de l'argent, **je construirais** une grande maison. (mais je n'ai pas d'argent) If I had money, I would build a big house. (but I don't have money)

Si j'avais une voiture, **j'irais** au travail en voiture.
If I had a car, I would drive to work. (but I don't have a car)

Si je connaissais son numéro de téléphone, **je lui téléphonerais**.
If I knew her phone number, I would call her. (I don't know it.)

Si j'étais à ta place – If I were you

Often used for giving advice:

Si j'étais à ta place, je ferais...
If I were you, I would do...

Si j'étais à ta place j'irais chez le dentiste tout de suite.
If I were you, I would go to the dentist straight away.

Qu'est-ce que tu ferais si... ?
What would you do, if...?

Qu'est-ce que tu ferais si tu étais Premier ministre ?
What would you do if you were Prime Minister?

2.<u>Condition with low probability</u> <u>in the future.</u>

Si je gagnais au loto, **je ferais** un tour du monde.
If I won the lottery, I would take a trip around the world.

Si j'obtenais le poste, **je pourrais** déménager plus proche du bureau.
If I got the job, I might move closer to the office.
S'il y avait une guerre, **nous serions obligés** de...
If there were a war, we would have to...
Même **si je lui demandais, elle ne me dirait rien.**
Even if I asked her, she would not tell me anything.

3 <u>**Speaking politely, giving advice, expressing a wish**</u>. (modal verbs)
Je voudrais un café, s'il vous plait.
I would like a cup of coffee, please.
Pourriez-vous m'aider, s'il vous plaît?
Could you help me, please?
Tu devrais parler avec ton chef.
You should talk to your boss.

You can find more about the use of **Conditionnel présent** with modal verbs in the next Unit.

<u>CONDITION IN THE PAST</u>

Si j'avais vu, j'aurais fait...

If I had had, I would have done...

Si + Plus-que-parfait ... , ...	**Conditionnel passé**
First part of the sentence:	Second part of the sentence:

We are talking about the past and what would have happened under certain condition (but did not happen).

Conditionnel passé

avoir/être (Conditionnel présent) + **participe passé**

avoir		être	
J'aurais	**nous aurions**	**Je serais**	**nous serions**
Tu aurais	**vous auriez**	**Tu serais**	**vous seriez**
il/elle aurait	**ils/elles auraient**	**Il/elle serait**	**ils/elles seraient**

The verbs conjugated with **être** in **Passé composé** and **Plus-que-parfait** are also conjugated with **être** in **Conditionnel passé** and their past participles agree with the subject in gender and number.

Si tu m'avais parlé du concert, **je serais venu(e)**.
If you had told me about the concert, I would have come. (but you did not tell me)

or j'aurais pu venir – I could have come

Si j'avais eu son numéro de téléphone, **je lui aurais téléphoné**.
If I had known her phone number, I would have called her. (but I did not know it)

or j'aurais pu l'appeler – I could have called her

Si j'avais mieux révisé, **j'aurais réussi** l'examen.
If I had studied harder, I would have passed the exam. (but I did not work hard)

Mixed Conditional

« Mixed » means in this case that one part of the sentence is an imaginary situation, different from reality, and the other part refers to the past.

Si j'avais fait des études à l'université, **j'aurais** un meilleur poste maintenant.
If I had studied at university (I didn't), I would have a better job now. (I don't).

Si j'avais du talent (mais je n'en ai pas), **je serais devenu** acteur.
If I had talent (I don't), I would have become an actor (I didn't).

EXERCISES **Conjugate the verbs:**

1. - Est-ce que tu … (venir) au concert des enfants ce samedi ? Are you going to come to the kids concert this Saturday?

- Je ne suis pas sûr. Si je … (être) encore occupé avec la conférence, je … (ne pas aller).
I'm not sure. If I am still busy with the work conference, I won't go.

…

2. - Tout ce que tu cuisines est délicieux ! Si tu .. (ouvrir) un restaurant, tu … (avoir) beaucoup de succès. Everything you cook is delicious! If you opened your own restaurant, you would have a great success.

- Si je … (ne pas aimer) mon travail autant, je … probablement (courir) le risque. If I did not love my job so much, I would probably have taken the risk.

…

3. - Où est mon sac bleu ? Je … le (chercher) depuis une heure ! Where is my blue bag? I have been looking for it for one hour!

- Je n'ai aucune idée. Si tu .. le (ne pas trouver), je … te (donner) le mien. I have no idea. If you do not find it, I will give you mine.

…

4. - Tu as vu cette offre d'emploi ? Si je … (être) à ta place, je … (candidater). Did you see this job ad? If I were you, I would apply for it.

- Ça semble intéressant, c'est vrai. Mais ils veulent quelqu'un ayant une maîtrise parfaite du français. Si mon francais … (être) meilleur, je … (avoir) plus de chance d'avoir le poste. It sounds interesting indeed. But they want someone with perfect French. If my French were better, I would have more chances of getting it.

…

5. - Pourquoi tu rentres si tard ? Why are you getting home so late?

- Eh bien, si tu … me (ne pas demander) de faire les courses, je … (rentrer) beaucoup plus tôt. Well, if you had not asked me to do the shopping, I would have got home much earlier.

…

6. - Est-ce que tu penses qu'il m'aime ? Do you think he loves me?

- Bien sûr qu'il t'aime ! S'il … te (ne pas aimer), il … te (ne pas épouser). Of course he does! If he did not love you, he would not have married you.

…

7. - Si tu … (ne pas mentir) à ta copine, tu … (ne pas avoir) d'ennuis maintenant. If you had not lied to your girlfriend, you would not be in trouble now.

- Je sais, arrête de me le rappeler ! I know, stop reminding me!

DIALOGUE « Appartement à louer »

Au bistrot avec Olivier.

Olivier : Salut, Peter, comment ça va ? On ne t'a pas vu depuis plus de deux semaines.

Peter : Salut, Olivier, ça fait plaisir de te revoir. J'ai été très occupé ces jours-ci, je travaille vraiment beaucoup. Et toi ?

Olivier : Moi, j'ai décidé de déménager, je suis en train de chercher un appartement à louer. J'en ai déjà vu quelques-uns, mais rien d'intéressant pour le moment. Je veux deux chambres à coucher et un garage. Il y a une annonce d'aujourd'hui, l'appartement semble pas mal sur les photos et je vais le voir demain. **S'il me plaît, je vais signer le contrat.**

Peter : J'espère qu'il va te plaire. Est-ce qu'il est proche d'un parc ?

Olivier : Oui, s'il **n'était pas, je n'aurais pas été intéressé**. Tu sais que je cours tous les matins.

Peter : Je sais, je le fais moi aussi. J'espère qu'il n'est pas loin de ton travail non plus. **Si moi, j'avais trouvé quelque chose de bien, plus proche de mon bureau, ça aurait été mieux.** Au moins je suis maintenant tout près du Bois de Vincennes et je peux courir dans la forêt.

Olivier : Super !

Olivier : Hi, Peter, how have you been? We haven't seen you for more than two weeks.

Peter : Hello, Olivier, nice to see you again. I've been very busy, working really hard. How about you?

Olivier : Well, I decided to move to another place, so I have been looking for a flat to rent. I have already seen a few apartments but nothing interesting until now. I want two bedrooms and a garage. There is one ad from today, the flat looks good in the photos and I am going to see it tomorrow. If I like it, I will sign the contract.

Peter : I hope you will. Is there a park nearby?

Olivier : Yes, if there were not, I would not be interested. You know I go jogging every morning.

Peter : I know, me too. I hope it is not far away from your work either. If I had found something good next to my office, it would have been better. At least I am now close to Bois de Vincennes and I can go jogging in the forest.

Olivier: Great!

USEFUL VOCABULARY : house, furniture

une propriété – property ; **de l'immobilier** – real estate ; **un immeuble** – building **un appartement** – flat / apartment ; **un rez-de-chaussée** – ground floor **le premier étage** – first floor ; **un ascenseur** – lift / elevator ; **une maison** – house **une maison de campagne** – cottage ; **un grenier** – attic ; **une cave** – basement

des voisins – neighbours ; **un ménage** – household

vendre – to sell ; **acheter** – to buy ; **louer** – to rent ; **un propriétaire** – landlord / owner ; **un locataire** – tenant

meublé – furnished ; **des meubles** – furniture

un chauffage central – central heating ; **une climatisation** – air conditioner

des factures – utility bills

un balcon – balcony ; **la cour** – yard ; **un jardin** – garden ; **un potager** – vegetable garden ; **des fleurs** – flowers ; **des arbres** – trees ; **de l'herbe** – grass ; **une pelouse** – lawn ; **tondre la pelouse / couper l'herbe** – to mow the lawns

une entrée – hall ; **un salon** – living room ; **une salle à manger** – dining room **une chambre à coucher** – bedroom ; **une cuisine** – kitchen ; **une salle de bains** – bathroom ; **une penderie, un placard** – closet

des fenêtres – windows ; **un mur** – wall ; **un plancher** – floor ; **un plafond** – ceiling

une cuisine équipée – fitted kitchen

des placards de cuisine – kitchen cupboards ; **un évier** – sink ; **un électroménager** – electric appliances ; **un frigo** – fridge ; **un congélateur** – freezer ; **une machine à café** – coffee machine ; **une cuisinière** – cooker ; **un four** – oven ; **des plaques** – hot-plates ; **un lave-vaisselle** – dishwasher ; **une machine à laver** – washing machine ; **une chaudière** – water heater ; **un sèche-linge** – dryer ; **sécher** – to dry **le linge** – laundry; **une pince à linge** – peg ; **un fer à repasser, repasser** – an iron, to iron ; **un aspirateur** – vacuum cleaner

une prise – plug ; **brancher** – to plug in ; **le bouton** – a switch ; **un câble** – cable **un fil de fer** – wire ; **un fusible** – safety fuse ; **une ampoule électrique** – light bulb

une chambre à coucher – bedroom

un lit – bed ; **un matelas** – mattress ; **une couverture** – blanket ; **des draps** – sheets **un oreiller** – pillow ; **une armoire** – wardrobe ; **un tiroir** – drawer ; **une commode** – chest of drawers ; **une table de nuit** – bedside table ; **des rideaux** – curtains **des stores** – blinds ; **un tapis** – carpet

un canapé – sofa ; **un fauteuil** – armchair ; **une table** – table ; **une biblio-thèque** – book case ; **des étagères** – book shelves ; **des tableaux** – paintings **une chaise** – chair ; **un lustre** – chandelier ; **un buffet** – sideboard ; **un bureau** – desk **une cheminée** – fireplace

une salle de bains – bathroom

un lavabo – wash basin ; **se laver** – to wash ; **un miroir** – mirror ; **une baignoire** – bath ; **une douche** – shower ; **prendre une douche** – have a shower ; **des serviettes** – towels

UNIT 19

SUBJONCTIF

Le Subjonctif in French is a specific verb form used with some impersonal expressions and some verbs which express feelings. It is much more often used than the Subjunctive in English.

HOW do we form it ?

> **The stem of 3ᵉ person plural au Présent (ils) + endings**

-e	-ions
-es	-iez
-e	-ent

verb I group	verb II group	verb III group
parler	**finir**	**repondre**
ils/elles **parl**-ent	ils/elles **finiss**-ent	ils/elles **repond**-ent
que je parl**e**	que je finiss**e**	que je repond**e**
que tu parl**es**	que tu finiss**es**	que tu repond**es**
qu'il/elle parl**e**	qu'il/elle finiss**e**	qu'il/elle repond**e**
que nous parl**ions**	que nous finiss**ions**	que nous repond**ions**
que vous parl**iez**	que vous finiss**iez**	que vous repond**iez**
qu'ils/elles parl**ent**	qu'ils/elles finiss**ent**	qu'ils/elles repond**ent**

Irregular verbs

avoir	etre	aller
que j'aie	que je sois	que j'aille
que tu aies	que tu sois	que tu ailles
qu'il/elle ait	qu'il/elle soit	qu'il/elle aille

que nous ayons	que nous soyons	que nous allions
que vous ayez	que vous soyez	que vous alliez
qu'ils/elles aient	qu'ils/elles soient	qu'ils/elles aillent

dire	**faire**	**savoir**
que je dise	que je fasse	que je sache
que tu dises	que tu fasses	que tu saches
qu'il/elle dise	qu'il/elle fasse	qu'il/elle sache
que nous disions	que nous fassions	que nous sachions
que vous disiez	que vous fassiez	que vous sachiez
qu'ils/elles disent	qu'ils/elles fassent	qu'ils/elles sachent

pouvoir	**devoir**	**vouloir**
que je puisse	que je doive	que je veuille
que tu puisses	que tu doives	que tu veuilles
qu'il/elle puisse	qu'il/elle doive	qu'il/elle veuille
que nous puissions	que nous devions	que nous voulions
que vous puissiez	que vous deviez	que vous vouliez
qu'ils/elles puissent	qu'ils/elles doivent	qu'ils/elles veuillent

Two verbs which are irregular only in the forms **nous** and **vous** (only one « n » instead of two):

prendre	**venir**
que je prenne	que je vienne
que tu prennes	que tu viennes
qu'il/elle prenne	qu'il/elle vienne
que nous prenions	**que nous venions**
que vous preniez	**que vous veniez**
qu'ils/elles prennent	qu'ils/elles viennent

Subjonctif passé

Refers to the past. You can find it mostly in written French and formal style speeches but sometimes even in everyday conversations.

parler	aller
que j'aie parlé	que je sois allé(e)
que tu aies parlé	que tu sois allé(e)
qu'il/elle ait parlé	qu'il soit allé /elle soit allée
que nous ayons parlé	que nous soyons allé(e)s
que vous ayez parlé	que vous soyez allé(e)s
qu'ils/elles aient parlé	qu'ils soient allés / qu'elles soient allées

WHEN
DO WE USE LE **SUBJONCTIF** ?

1. After <u>impersonal expressions</u>: **il faut que, il suffit que, il arrive que, il est nécessaire, il est possible/probable, c'est dommage:**

<u>Il faut</u> **que tu ailles** à la mairie. You must go to the municipality.

<u>C'est dommage</u> **qu'ils ne soient pas** avec nous maintenant. It is a pity they are not with us now.

<u>Il est important</u> **que vous veniez** à cette réunion. It is important that you come to this meeting.

<u>C'est bien</u> **que tu sois venu** à la fête. It is good that you have come to the party. (Subjonctif passé)

2. After verbs which express <u>feelings</u>, (joy, sadness, desire, doubt, fear) – **vouloir, demander, désirer, souhaiter, préférer, douter, regretter, craindre, avoir peur, être content (heureux/triste/surpris)** when there are **two different** subjects in the sentence.

Je <u>préfère</u> **que tu viennes** avec nous.
I prefer that you come with us.

Le directeur <u>demande</u> **que j'aille** à cette conférence.
The boss has asked me to go to this conference.

Je suis **heureux que tu sois** avec moi.
I am happy that you are with me.

If the subject is the same (it performs both actions in the sentence), we will not need a Subjunctif:
<u>Je préfère venir</u> avec vous.
I prefer to come with you.
<u>Il demande d'aller</u> à cette conférence.
He has asked to go to this conference.
<u>Je suis heureux d'être</u> avec toi.
I am happy to be with you.

    3. After the verbs **croire, penser, trouver** in <u>negative form</u>:

<u>Je ne pense pas</u> **qu'il soit** compétant sur ce sujet.
I do not think he is competent on this subject.

<u>Je ne crois pas</u> **que nous devions** demander un visa.
I do not think that we have to apply for a visa.

    4. After some conjunctions like **avant que, pour que, bien que, sans que, quoique:**

J'essaye de bien expliquer <u>pour que</u> **vous puissiez** tout comprendre.
I am trying to explain well so that you can understand everything.

<u>Quoiqu</u>**'elle ait reçu** un Oscar, elle reste une personne modeste.
Even though she has an Oscar, she remains a humble person.

Je sais conduire <u>bien que</u> **je n'aie pas** encore de permis.
I can drive although I haven't got a license yet.

UNIT 20

VERBES MODAUX

There is no unanimity among linguistic experts about modal verbs in French. As we always try to make a comparison between English and French and to find a correspondence between grammatical structures, we are going to follow the experts who consider three French verbs to be modal: **pouvoir**, **devoir** and **falloir**. They correspond to the English modal verbs can, could, must, should, might, may.

While in English there are a lot of subtle nuances in the use of modal verbs, things in French in this area are easier and simpler.

What is a modal verb?

Modal verbs allow us to express possibility, capacity, obligation, permission. They are also used to make deduction with various degrees of probability.

They are auxiliary verbs – that is to say they cannot stay alone in the sentence and are always followed by another verb.

POUVOIR

Présent	Passé composé	Imparfait	Plus-que-parfait
je peux	j'ai pu	je pouvais	j'avais pu
tu peux	tu as pu	tu pouvais	tu avais pu
il/elle peut	il/elle a pu	il/elle pouvait	il/elle avait pu
nous pouvons	nous avons pu	nous pouvions	nous avions pu
vous pouvez	vous avez pu	vous pouviez	vous aviez pu
ils/elles peuvent	ils/elles ont pu	ils/elles pouvaient	ils/elles avaient pu

Futur simple	Conditionnel présent	Conditionnel passé	Subjonctif
je pourrai	je pourrais	j'aurais pu	que je puisse
tu pourras	tu pourrais	tu aurais pu	que tu puisses
il/elle pourra	il/elle pourrait	il/elle aurait pu	qu'il/elle puisse

nous pourrons	nous pourrions	nous aurions pu	que nous puissions
vous pourrez	vous pourriez	vous auriez pu	que vous puissiez
ils/elles pourront	ils/elles pourraient	ils/elles auraient pu	qu'ils/elles puissent

<u>Pouvoir au Présent – je peux, tu peux...</u>
<u>Translated by **can, may**</u>

1. <u>Capacity</u>

Il peut parler espagnol. He can speak Spanish.

2. <u>Possibility</u>

Nous pouvons voir la montagne de notre chambre d'hôtel. We can see the mountain from our hotel room.

3. <u>Permission / asking for permission</u>

- giving permission

Si tu as besoin d'un dictionnaire, **tu peux utiliser** le mien. If you need a dictionary, you can use mine.

- asking for permission

Est-ce que je peux fumer ici ? Can I smoke here?

4. <u>Asking</u>

Est-ce que tu peux me passer le sel s'il te plaît ? Can you pass me the salt please?

Est-ce que je peux avoir un verre d'eau ? Can I have a glass of water?

Tu peux m'aider ? Can you help me?

Est-ce que je peux entrer ? May I come in?

Est-ce que je peux vous rappeler plus tard ? May I call you later?

Pouvoir au Conditionnel présent – je pourrais, tu pourrais...

Translated by **could**

1. Asking

Tu pourrais...? ((more polite option than **Tu peux...?**)

Tu pourrais me prêter un peu d'argent ? Could you lend me some money?

Pourriez-vous m'envoyer un peu plus d'informations? Could you send me some more information?

2. Suggestion

Tu pourrais... Nous pourrions...

Qu'est-ce qu'on fait ce weekend ? What shall we do this weekend?

On pourrait aller à la montagne. We could go to the mountain.

Quand tu reviens en France la prochaine fois, **on pourrait organiser** une réunion d'anciens élèves.
When you come to France next time, we could organize a classmate reunion.

3. Situation imaginaire

Cette île est splendide ! **Je pourrais rester** vivre ici pour toujours.
This island is lovely! I could stay and live here forever.

Je ne pourrais pas vivre à la campagne. Je suis habitué à la grande ville.
I couldn't live in the country. I am used to the big city.

Je suis très content de cette décision. **Ça ne pourrait pas être mieux.**
I'm very pleased with this decision. It couldn't be better.

Pouvoir au Passé Composé – j'ai pu, je n'ai pas pu...

Translated by **managed to, couldn't**

Talking about a particular moment in the past:

J'ai pu envoyer l'argent avant que la banque ne ferme.
I managed to send the money before the bank closed.

J'ai finalement pu le convaincre.
I finally managed to persuade him.

Je n'ai pas pu prendre le bus à 5 heures. J'ai été retenu au travail.
I couldn't catch the bus at 5pm. I was held up at work.

<u>Pouvoir à l'Imparfait</u> – **je pouvais, tu pouvais**...

<u>Translated by</u> **could** (<u>the past of can</u>)

Talking about a skill we had in the past:

Je pouvais nager quand j'avais 5 ans. I could swim when I was five.

Il pouvait lire avant d'aller à l'école. He could read before he started going to school.

<u>DEVOIR</u>

Présent	Passé composé	Imparfait	Plus-que-parfait
je dois	j'ai dû	je devais	j'avais dû
tu dois	tu as dû	tu devais	tu avais dû
il/elle doit	il/elle a dû	il/elle devait	il/elle avait dû
nous devons	nous avons dû	nous devions	nous avions dû
vous devez	vous avez dû	vous deviez	vous aviez dû
ils/elles doivent	ils/elles ont dû	ils/elles devaient	ils/elles avaient dû

Futur simple	Conditionnel présent	Conditionnel passé	Subjonctif
je devrai	je devrais	j'aurais dû	que je doive
tu devras	tu devrais	tu aurais dû	que tu doives
il/elle devra	il/elle devrait	il/elle aurait dû	qu'il/elle doive
nous devrons	nous devrions	nous aurions dû	que nous devions
vous devrez	vous devriez	vous auriez dû	que vous deviez
ils/elles devront	ils/elles devraient	ils/elles auraient dû	qu'ils/elles doivent

Devoir au Présent – je dois, tu dois... = must

1. **Obligation**

Tu dois ranger ta chambre. You must tidy your room.

Je dois terminer le rapport d'ici demain. You must finish this report by tomorrow.

2. **Strong recommendation**, advice

Tu dois voir ce film ! You **must see** this film!

Devoir au Passé composé – j'ai dû, tu as dû... = had to

J'ai dû aller à la poste hier pour récupérer mon colis.
Yesterday I had to go to the post office to get my parcel.

Devoir à l'Imparfait – je devais, tu devais... = was supposed to

Je devais aller à la poste office hier pour récupérer mon colis, mais j'ai oublié.
I was supposed to go to the post yesterday, but I forgot.

Nous devions participer à la conférence, mais le programme a changé.
We were supposed to take part in the conference, but the schedule changed.

Devoir au Conditionnel présent – je devrais, tu devrais...= should

Giving advice

Tu devrais lire ce livre. You should read this book.

Often combined with:

Je pense / Je ne pense pas que tu devrais...

Je pense que **tu devrais postuler** à ce poste. I think you should apply for this job.

FALLOIR (il faut) = must / have to / need

Falloir is an impersonal verb and all its forms start with **Il**.

Present	Passé composé	Imparfait	Plus-que-parfait
Il faut	il a fallu	il fallait	il avait fallu

Futur simple	Conditionnel present	Conditionnel passé	Subjonctif
Il faudra	il faudrait	il aurait fallu	qu'il faille

(-) Il ne faut pas
(?) Est-ce qu'il faut ?

Falloir can mean **devoir** (obligation) or **avoir besoin** (need).

- Il faut + infinitif

Often used when we talk about things in general, or when the subject is « we ».

Il faut respecter la loi. One has to respect the law.

Il ne faut pas jeter des ordures dans la rue. You must not throw litter in the street.

Il faut se dépêcher. = Nous devons nous dépêcher. We must hurry.

- Il faut + que + Subjonctif

Il faut que vous reveniez demain. = Vous devez revenir demain.
You should come back tomorrow.

Il faut que tu ailles chez le dentiste. = Tu dois aller chez le dentiste.
You must go to the dentist.

Il fallait que je règle ce problème. = Je devais régler ce problème.
I had to fix this problem.

- Il + pronom + faut + nom.
Il me faut un bon livre pour apprendre l'espagnol.
I need a good book to study Spanish.

Il vous faudra de l'argent pour commencer ce business.
You will need some money to start this business.

Il lui faudrait un peu d'aide.
He would need a bit of help.

Modal verbs – Probability

Pouvoir and **devoir** can be used to make a deduction and express probability. It is far easier than in English where *must, could, might, may, should* can be combined with different infinitives and express a lot of nuances.

In French there are only two types of infinitives: **Present** and **Past**.

Past infinitive (infinitif passé):

avoir (or **être**) + **participe passé**

> parler   → **avoir parlé**
> dire   → **avoir dit**
> aller   → **être allé(es)**

When the auxiliary is **être**, the past participle agrees with the subject.

DEVOIR

> **- au Présent (je dois, tu dois...) = must**

Ils sortent souvent le soir. **Ils doivent avoir beaucoup d'amis.**
They often go out in the evening. They must have a lot of friends.

Tu n'as rien mangé toute la journée, **tu dois avoir faim** !
You haven't eaten anything all day, you must be hungry!

> **- au Conditionnel présent (je devrais, tu devrais...) = should**

Les invités **devraient arriver** bientôt. Our guests should arrive soon.

Cet exercice ne devrait pas te prendre beaucoup de temps. This exercise shouldn't take you too long.

Il devrait y avoir encore des sandwichs. There should be some sandwiches left.

> **- au Passé composé (j'ai dû, tu as dû ...) = should have** (probability about the past)

Elle a dû bien réussir l'examen. She should have done well on the test.

Il a dû oublier de m'appeler. He must have forgotten to call me.

> **- au Conditionnel Passé (j'aurait dû, tu aurais dû ...) = should have** (reproach or regret)

Tu aurais dû acheter de la viande. You should have bought some meat.

Tu n'aurais pas dû dire à Tom. You shouldn't have told Tom.

Tu aurais dû venir à la fête, c'était super ! You should have come to the party, it was great!

Je n'aurais pas dû laisser la fenêtre ouverte. I shouldn't have left the window open.

Je n'aurais pas dû manger autant, je ne me sens pas bien !
I shouldn't have eaten so much.
I feel sick now!

POUVOIR

> **- au Présent (je peux, tu peux...) = may / might / could**

On peut aller en Italie cet été. We might go to Italy this summer.

Je peux t'appeler plus tard, ça dépend à quelle heure je finis le travail. I might give you a ring later, it depends on what time I finish work.

Ils peuvent arriver à chaque instant. They could be here at any moment.

Tu peux avoir raison. You could be right.

> **- au Présent (je peux, tu peux) + infinitif passé = might have / could have**

Ils peuvent avoir décidé de rester. They might have decided to stay.

Il peut avoir parlé avec elle. He may have talked to her.

Ils peuvent avoir pris le train plus tôt. They could have caught the early train.

- **au Conditionnel passé (j'aurais pu, tu aurais pu...) = could have**

Tu aurais pu demander au professeur de t'aider. You could have asked the teacher for help.

Pourquoi tu as touché la plaque ?! **Tu aurais pu te brûler**. Why did you touch the cooker?! You could have burnt yourself.

- **à la forme négative (ça ne peut pas, ne pouvait pas) = can't be, can't have been**

Cette veste ne peut pas être à Peter, elle est trop petite ! This coat can't be Peter's. It is too small!

Il ne peut pas dormir, il est à peine 20 heures. He can't be sleeping, it is only 8 pm.

Elle ne pouvait pas être au bureau hier. Elle est en voyage d'affaires. She can't have been in the office yesterday. She is on a business trip.

EXERCISES   Conjugate the verbs:

1. - Je ... (ne pas pouvoir) venir *ce* soir. Je ... (devoir) réviser pour mon examen. I can't come out tonight. I have to study for my exam.

- Allez ! Tu ... (devoir) te reposer de temps en temps. Come on! You must have a break from time to time.

...

2. - Est-ce que je ... (pouvoir) te parler ? Can I have a word with you?

- Bien sûr, je me libère dans environ une heure. Nous ... (pouvoir) aller déjeuner ensemble, si tu veux. Sure, I will be free in about an hour. We can go for lunch together if you want.

...

3. – Tu ... (devoir) te lever tôt demain. ... (ne pas falloir) que tu... (veiller) ce soir. You must get up early tomorrow. You shouldn't stay late tonight.

- Ne t'inquiète pas, je ne vais pas tarder. Don't worry, I won't.

...

4. - Je ... (devoir) laver la voiture hier, mais je n'ai pas eu de temps. I was supposed to wash the car yesterday, but I didn't have time.

- **Pas de soucis, tu … (pouvoir) la laver demain matin.** Don't worry, you can wash it tomorrow morning.

5. - Où sont les ciseaux ? Where are the scissors?

- **Ils … (devoir) être dans le premier tiroir.** They should be in the top drawer.

…

6. – Je … (ne pas pouvoir) trouver le chat. I can't find the cat.

- **Il … (pouvoir) se cacher derrière l'armoire.** He might be hiding behind the wardrobe.

…

7. - Est-ce que les enfants sont à l'école ? Are the children at school?

- **Non. Ils … (devoir) être en train de jouer dans le parc.** No, they aren't. They must be playing in the park.

…

8. - Tu … (ne pas devoir) dire à Louise pour la fête ! C'était un secret.
You shouldn't have told Louise about the party! It was a secret.

- **C'est pas moi qui lui ai dit ! Sarah … (devoir) lui dire.** I did not tell her! Sarah must have told her.

…

9. – Je … (devoir) aller à la banque ce matin pour envoyer de l'argent à ma mère. I had to go to the bank this morning to send some money to my mother.

- **Tu … (pouvoir) l'envoyer en ligne. C'est tellement plus facile.**
You could have sent it online. It is so much easier.

DIALOGUE « Dinner with Julie and Kate »

Peter, who knows nothing about cooking, has tried to make « une tartiflette » for his sister and Julie.

Julie : Ça sent bon, mais le goût est bizarre…

Julie: It smells nice, but it has a strange taste...

Peter : Hm, oui, j'ai peur d'avoir fait une erreur. **Il ne devrait pas être** comme ça. **J'ai dû mettre** trop de sel.

Peter: Hm yes, I'm afraid there is something wrong, it shouldn't taste like this. I must have put too much salt.

Kate : Non, je ne pense pas que ce soit trop salé. Est-ce que tu as mis tout selon la recette ?

Kate: No, I don't think it's too salty. Did you put everything according to the recipe?

Peter : Euhh, je dois admettre que je n'ai pas de recette. J'avais lu quelque part comment faire et j'ai fait confiance à ma mémoire. **J'aurais dû chercher un bon site de cuisine sur Internet.**

Peter: Well... I must admit I don't have a recipe. I had read something about it and I relied on my memory. I guess I should have searched for a good cooking site on the Internet.

Julie : Ne t'inquiète pas. **On peut tout de même le manger.**

Julie: Don't worry. We can still eat it.

Peter : Heureusement nous avons un bon dessert. Une crème brûlée. C'est une surprise spéciale pour ma sœur.

Peter: The good thing is that there is a nice dessert. It is called Crème brûlée. It is a special surprise for my sister.

Kate : Super ! **Est-ce que nous pouvons goûter** à cette fameuse crème ?

Kate: Great ! Can we try this famous Crème?

Peter : Bien sûr, là voici.

Peter: Sure, here you are.

Julie : Tu ne trouves pas que le goût est un peu bizarre ?

Julie: Don't you think that the taste is a bit strange?

Peter : Oh non, **j'ai dû faire** une autre bêtise !

Peter: Oh no, I must have done something silly again!

USEFUL VOCABULARY : food, cooking

Food

Attention!

Some food products are uncountable and take the « article partitif » – **du, de la**.

de la viande – meat ; **du porc** – pork ; **du veau** – beef ; **de l'agneau** – lamb **du poulet** – chicken ; **de la dinde** – turkey ; **du gibier** – game

du poisson -fish ; **des fruits de mer** – sea food ; **des huîtres** – oysters ; **des moules** - mussels / clams ; **des crevettes** – shrimps

des œufs – eggs ; **des produits laitiers** – dairy products ; **du lait** – milk ; **du beurre** - butter ; **de la crème fraîche** – cream ; **du fromage** – cheese

des légumes – vegetables ; **une tomate** – tomato ; **un poivron** – pepper ; **un piment** - chilly pepper ; **des pommes de terre** – potatoes ; **un chou** – cabbage ; **une carotte** – carrot ; **une betterave** – beetroot ; **un gingembre** – ginger ; **des épinards** – spinach **un chou-fleur** – cauliflower ; **de l'ail** – garlic ; **un oignon** – onion ; **une courgette** - zucchini ; **des haricots verts** – string beans ; **des champignons** – mushrooms

une citrouille – pumpkin

des légumineux – legumes ; **des haricots** – beans ; **des petit pois** – pea
des lentilles – lentils

des herbes – herbs ; **des épices** – spices

des fruits – fruit ; **une pomme** – apple ; **une poire** – pear ; **une prune** – plum
des cerises – cherries ; **des fraises** – strawberries ; **des framboises** – raspberries
des mûres – blackberries ; **des myrtilles** – blueberries ; **des canneberges** - cranberries ; **une pêche** – peach ; **un abricot** – apricot ; **du raisin** – grapes
un melon – melon ; **une pastèque** – watermelon ; **un citron** – lemon
un pamplemousse – grapefruit ; **un ananas** – pineapple

des fruits secs – nuts ; **une noix** – walnut ; **une noisette** – hazelnut ; **une amande** - almond ; **une cacahuète** – peanut ; **un marron** – chestnut

des céréales – cereals ; **du blé** – wheat ; **du riz** – rice ; **de l'avoine** – oat flakes

de la farine – flour ; **du sucre** – sugar ; **de la pâte** – pastry ; **du miel** – honey

de l'huile d'olive – olive oil ; **de l'huile de tournesol** – sunflower oil ; **de l'huile de colza** – canola oil

<u>In the kitchen</u>

des couverts – cutlery ; **une fourchette** – fork ; **une cuillère** – spoon ; **une cuillère de thé** – tea spoon ; **un couteau** – knife

un verre – glass ; **une tasse** – cup ; **un verre de vin** – glass of wine ; **une tasse de thé / de café** – cup of tea / cup of coffee

un tire-bouchon – corkscrew ; **une salière** – salt cellar/shaker ; **des balances** – scales ; **une nappe** – tablecloth

bouillir – to boil ; **cuire à la vapeur** – to stew ; **mijoter** – to simmer ; **frire** – to fry
dorer – to brown ; **faire cuire un gâteau au four** – to bake a cake ; **faire cuire de la viande au four** – to roast ; **griller** – to grill

trancher – to slice ; **couper en morceaux / hacher** – to chop ; **peler** – to peel
couper – to cut ; **râper** – to grate ; **remuer** – to stir ; **presser** – to squeeze
saupoudrer – to sprinkle ; **mélanger** – to mix ; **un mélange** – mixture

brûler – to burn ; **coller** – to stick

une casserole – saucepan / pot ; **une poêle** – frying pan ; **un bol** – bowl

UNIT 21

DISCOURS INDIRECT

Le discours indirect (indirect speech) allows us to report what someone else has said.

If Peter says, for example:

- **J'ai été** en Espagne.
- I have been to Spain. (direct speech)

Peter a dit **qu'il avait été** en Espagne.
Peter said (that) he had been to Spain. (indirect speech)

Note that in the indirect speech « **j'ai été** » has become « **il avait été** »

In difference with English, the particle « **que** » which corresponds to « that » cannot be omitted.

Elle a dit **qu'**elle allait m'appeler plus tard.
She said she would call me later.

To turn direct speech to indirect:

- Change the pronoun – switch from « je » to « il/elle »
- Change the verb tense – shift it back.
- Change the time.

avoir and **être** from direct to indirect speech:

je suis → **il/elle était**

j'ai　　→ **il/elle avait**

Il a dit : « **Je suis** fatigué ». Il a dit **qu'il était** fatigué.

He said: « I am tired ». He said that he was tired.

(« je **suis** » becomes «il **était** »)

Il a dit : « **J'ai** un rendez-vous ». Il a dit **qu'il avait** un rendez-vous.

He said: « I have an appoinement ». He said that he had an appointment.

(«**j'ai** » becomes «**il avait** »)

Change of the verb tenses:

Présent → Imparfait

« **Je veux** venir avec toi. » Il a dit **qu'il voulait** venir avec moi.

« I want to come with you. » He said that he wanted to come with me.

Je suis en train de… → **il était en train de**…

« **Je suis en train de faire** une pizza. » Il a dit **qu'il était en train de faire** une pizza.

« I am cooking a pizza. » He said he was cooking a pizza.

Passé composé → Plus-que-parfait

« **J'ai acheté** un nouvel ordinateur. » Il a dit **qu'il avait acheté** un nouvel ordinateur.

« I have bought a new computer. » He said (that) he had bought a new computer.

« **J'ai vu** Maria hier. » Il a dit **qu'il avait vu** Maria la veille.

« I saw Maria yesterday. » He said (that) he had seen Maria the day before.

Je viens de … → il venait de…

« **Je viens de rentrer**. » Il a dit **qu'il venait de rentrer**.

« I just got home. » He said that he had just got home.

Futur simple → Futur dans le passé (= Conditionnel présent)

« **Je prendrai** probablement le bus .» Il a dit **qu'il prendrait** probablement le bus.

I'll probably take the bus. He said he would probably take the bus.

Je vais … → il allait…

« **Je vais** probablement **accepter** le poste ». Il a dit **qu'il allait** probablement **accepter** le poste.

« I will probably accept the job offer ». He said that he would probably accept the job offer.

When we report someone's words, we cannot use « aujourd'hui » (today), « hier » (yesterday) or « demain » (tomorrow), because these adverbs refer to the present. In the indirect speech, we use others.

Direct speech	Indirect speech
aujourd'hui "Je suis très occupé aujourd'hui."	**ce jour-là** – that day Il a dit qu'il était très occupé ce jour-là.
hier / hier soir "Je l'ai vu hier."	**la veille** – the day before Il a dit qu'il l'avait vu la veille.
demain "Je vais t'appeler demain."	**le lendemain** – the next day Elle a dit qu'elle allait m'appeler le lendemain.
la semaine prochaine "J'ai un rendez-vous la semaine prochaine."	**la semaine suivante** – the following week Il a dit qu'il avait un rendez-vous la semaine suivante.
la semaine passée "J'étais en vacances la semaine passée."	**la semaine précédente** – the previous week Il a dit qu'il avait été en vacances la semaine précédente.
maintenant	**alors** – then
il y a	**avant** – before
dans	**après** – later

When you are talking about something permanent you do not need to shift the verb tense back, you can keep the present.

« L'Italie **est** membre de l'Union européenne ».
« Italy is a member of the European Union ».

Il a dit que l'Italie **est** membre de l'Union européenne.
He said that Italy is a member of the European Union.

Demande/request – with the particle « **de** » and the infinitive:

« Est-ce que tu peux m'envoyer le rapport ? » Elle m'a demandé **de lui envoyer** le rapport.

« Could you send me the report, please? » She asked me to send her the report.

If the sentence is in negative form, the negative particles « **ne...pas** » come after « **de** »

« Ne m'attendez pas ». Il nous a dit **de ne pas l'attendre**.

« Don't wait for me ». He told us not to wait for him.

Indirect speech – questions

➥ When there is no question word (quand, où, pourquoi, etc.) we use « **si** » which means whether/if.

Tu as été en France ? Il m'a demandé **si j'ai été** en France.
Have you been to France? He asked me if I had been to France.

Est-ce que tu continues à jouer au volleyball ? Il m'a demandé **si je continuais** à jouer au volleyball.
Do you still play volleyball? He asked me if I still played volleyball.

➥ When there is a question word, it links the two parts of the sentence (no need of « si »).

Où est-ce qu'elle habite ? Il m'a demandé où elle habite.

Where does she live? He asked me **where she lives**.

Quand est-ce que tu es arrivé ? Il m'a demandé **quand j'étais arrivé**.

When did you arrive? He asked me when I (had) arrived.

Indirect questions

Indirect questions are those introduced by:

Est-ce que tu sais... ? Est-ce que tu as une idée... ? Pouvez-vous me dire... ?

Word order following these introducing expressions is the same as in an affirmative sentence.

Est-ce que tu sais où elle prend ses cours de danse ?
Do you know where she goes to dancing classes?

A direct question would be:

Où est-ce qu'elle prend ses cours de danse ?
Where does she go to dancing classes?

Quelle heure est-il ? (direct question with inversion) What is the time?

Pouvez-vous me dire quelle heure il est ?
(indirect question, no inversion) Could you tell me what the time is?

Sentences of this kind often start with « **Je me demande** », « **Je ne suis pas sûr** », « **Je ne sais pas** »:

Je me demande si nos collègues de Prague vont venir à la réunion.
I wonder if our collegues from Prague will come to the meeting.

Je ne suis pas sûr à quelle heure le film commence.
I'm not sure what time the film starts.

Je n'ai aucune idée de pourquoi Kim a quitté son travail.
I have no idea why Kim has left her job.

QUI, QUE, QUOI, DONT, OU
RELATIVE PRONOUNS

➡ **Qui** – who, which (refers to a person or to thing which is the <u>**subject**</u> of the sentence)

C'est l'homme **qui** peut t'aider. This is the man who can help you.

J'aime les films **qui** finissent bien. I like movies which have happy endings.

Do we have to put a comma before « qui »?

In the examples above there is no comma because the information introduced by the pronoun « qui » is a defining clause. If we remove it, the sentence would not be clear.

If the clause introduced by « qui » is non-defining (only gives some additional information), we must put a comma:

C'est Ed King, **qui** travaille pour la BBC. This is Ed King, who works for the BBC.

➥ **Que** – that, which (refers to a person or to thing which is the **direct object** of the sentence (without preposition). The direct object is called in French « complément direct ».

La fille **que** je voulais voir n'était pas venue à la fête.
The girl (that) I wanted to see was not at the party.

C'est l'imprimante **que** nous avons achetée hier.
This is the printer (which) we bought yesterday.

Est-ce que c'est le livre **que** tu cherchais ?
Is this the book (that) you were looking for?

Attention!

« Que » <u>cannot</u> be omitted! (as « that » and « which » in English can)

➥ **Qui** with a preposition – can **only** refer **to people**

C'est le garçon **avec qui** je travaille. This is the boy I work with.

➥ **Quoi** with a preposition – can **only** refer **to things**

Il ne m'a pas dit **à quoi** il pensait. He did not tell me what he was thinking about.

Ce qui, ce que, dont

These relative pronouns do not refer to a single word but rather to an entire clause.

➥ **Ce qui** – what (refers to the subject in the sentence)

Ils ne savent pas **ce qui** s'était passé. They do not know what had happened.

➥ **Ce que** – what (refers to the object in the sentence)

Je n'ai pas compris **ce que** tu m'as dit. I didn't understand what you told me.

➥ **Dont** – a specific French pronoun used with a verb, an adjective or a noun which takes the preposition « **de** ».

Il y a tout **ce dont** nous avons besoin. (avoir besoin **de**)
There is everything we need.

Ce dont ils sont fièrs, c'est le succès de leur fille.(fier **de**)
What they are proud of is their's daughter success.

  où ; là où – where
Je veux vivre dans un pays **où** la loi est respectée.
I would like to live in a country where the law is respected.

  quand ; au moment où – when
J'étais étudiante à l'université **quand** j'ai fait connaissance avec lui.
I was a student at university when I met him.

Lequel

This pronoun is variable, it agrees in gender and number with the word it refers to.

	singular	plural
masculine	**lequel**	**lesquels**
feminine	**laquelle**	**lesquelles**

Lequel and its forms are often used with a preposition (**pour, sur, avec, dans**, etc.)

Il y a plusieurs raisons **pour lesquelles** j'ai refusé l'offre.
There are several reasons why I refused the offer.

Le mur **sur lequel** ils avaient écrit était repeint.
The wall where they had written was repainted.

When the preposition is « **de** » or « **à** », some new combined pronouns are formed.

preposition	masculine	feminine	masc. plural	fem. plural
de	**duquel**	**de laquelle**	**desquels**	**desquelles**
à	**auquel**	**à laquelle**	**auxquels**	**auxquelles**

Le séminaire **auquel** nous devions participer était annulé.
The workshop to which we were supposed to go was cancelled.

Il y a eu des élections **à la suite desquelles** on a changé le gouvernement.
There were elections after which they changed the government.

UNIT 22

LINKING WORDS
ET, PARCE QUE, MALGRÉ...

The « linking words » (conjunctions) are invariable words which serve to connect two nouns or groups of nouns.

Conjunctions can express:

↪ **Union**:

et – and ; **aussi** – also / too ; **également** – as well

en plus – besides

de plus – furthermore

↪ **Opposition**

mais – but

pourtant, cependant – however

Le travail n'était pas très intéressant. **Cependant**, c'était bien payé.

The job was not very interesting. However, the pay was good.

bien que – although

Bien qu'il commence à pleuvoir, on va aller se promener.

Although it is starting to rain, we will go for a walk.

malgré – despite / in spite of

Malgré la pluie on va aller se promener. Despite the rain we will go for a walk.

malgré le fait que – in spite of the fact that

Malgré le fait qu'elle disposait de la qualification nécessaire, elle n'a pas obtenu le poste.

In spite of the fact that she had the necessary qualification, she did not get the job.

au lieu de ; à la place de – instead of

Au lieu de travailler, j'ai regardé un film à la télé.
Instead of studying I watched a film on the TV.

Je peux aller **à ta place**, si tu veux. I can go instead of you if you want.

d'un autre côté – on the other hand ; **au contraire** – on the contrary

↪ <u>Cause</u>

parce que – because

Hier soir je suis allé me coucher tôt, **parce que j'étais** très fatigué.
Last night I went to bed early because I was very tired.

comme ; puisque – as / since

Comme les routes étaient bloquées, un hélicoptère a secouru les gens.
As the roads were blocked, a helicopter rescued the people.

à cause de – because of

Le concert a été reporté **à cause d'une pluie forte**.
The concert was put off because of the heavy rain.

en raison de / dû à (written language) – due to / owing to / on account of

Le problème est dû à leur niveau de vie plus faible.
The problem is due to their lower living standards.

↪ <u>Conséquence</u>

ainsi ; donc – so

c'est pourquoi – that's why

par conséquent (written language) – therefore

Votre expérience est un vrai atout pour l'entreprise. **Nous avons décidé par conséquent** de vous accorder une promotion. Your experience has been an asset for the company. We have therefore decided to promote you.

↪ <u>But</u>

Pour / en vue de – to + infinitive

Il a beaucoup travaillé **pour réussir** l'examen. He worked hard to pass the exam.

de ne pas – not to

On a décidé **de ne pas aller** à cette réunion. We decided not to go to that meeting.

afin de – in order to

en cas de – in case of

En cas d'incendie ne prenez pas l'ascenseur. In case of fire, do not use the elevator.

→ **Comparaison**

par exemple – for example

ou – or ; **soit … soit** – either … or ; **ni … ni** – neither … nor

comme – like / as

Parfois il se comporte **comme un enfant**. He sometimes behaves like a child.

comme ça – like this

Il faut le faire **comme ça**. You should do it like this.

Ils ont tout laissé **comme c'était** avant leur arrivée. They left everything as it was before their arrival.

Expressions

comme tu sais – as you know ; **comme je t'avais dit** – as I told you

comme tu veux – as you like ; **comme d'habitude** – as usual

tel que – such as

Certains animaux sauvages, **tels que** l'ours et le chimpanzé, sont menacés d'extinction. Some wild animals, such as the bear or chimpanzee, are endangered.

en tant que + profession

Elle travaille en Angleterre **en tant qu'infirmière**. She works in England as a nurse.

comme si – as if

Tu parles **comme si tu venais de te réveiller**. You sound as if you have just woken up.

Arrête de me traiter **comme si j'étais un enfant**. Stop treating me as if I were a child.

il semble, il paraît – it looks like / it looks as though

Il semble qu'il va pleuvoir. It looks like it's going to rain.

Il paraît qu'ils vont se marier bientôt.
It looks like they are going to get married soon.

à la différence de – unlike

A la différence de l'aérobic, les cours de callanetics ne sont pas aussi fatigants.
Unlike aerobics, callanetics is not so demanding.

au fait – by the way

Il fait terriblement chaud aujourd'hui… **Au fait**, comment ça s'est passé ton week-end à la montagne ?
It is terribly hot today… By the way, how was your weekend at the mountains?

en fait ; en réalité – in fact / actually

Tout le monde pense qu'il a un caractère difficile, **mais en fait** il est une très bonne personne.
Everyone thinks he has a bad temper, but in fact he is a very good person.

de toute façon ; quand-même – anyway

De toute façon, tu ne peux pas faire ça sans consulter tes collègues.
Anyway, you cannot do this without consulting your colleagues.

Il pleut, mais on va sortir **quand-même**. It is raining, but we'll go out anyway.

après tout – after all

Ne sois pas si sévère avec lui. Il est encore un enfant **après tout**.
Don't be too hard on him. After all, he is still a child.

dans l'ensemble – as a whole

Le travail est bon **dans l'ensemble**. The job is good as a whole.

au moins – at least

Je serai en voyage d'affaires à Madrid, mais **j'espère avoir au moins** une soirée libre. I'll be on a business trip in Madrid but I hope to have at least one evening free.

autrement dit – in other words

surtout – especially

évidemment – obviously

<u>Linking words</u> – <u>Summary</u>

Sequence – Ordre	**Result – Conséquence**
• Premièrement	• Donc
• Deuxièmement	• Comme résultat
• Finalement	• En conséquence de
• De plus	• Par conséquent
• En complément	• Ainsi
• Aussi	• D'où
• En conclusion	• Dû à
• En résumé	• En définitive
Emphasis – Mettre l'accent	**Addition – Union**
• Vraiment	• Et
• Evidemment	• De plus
• Manifestement	• Aussi
• En général	• Egalement
• En fait	
• Particulièrement	
• Précisément	
• Naturellement	

Reason – Cause	**Example – Exemple**
<ul><li>Parce que</li><li>Comme</li><li>En raison de</li><li>Du fait de</li></ul>	<ul><li>Par exemple</li><li>En l'occurrence</li><li>C'est-à-dire</li><li>Tel que</li><li>Y compris</li><li>A savoir</li></ul>
Contrast – Contraste	**Comparison – Comparaison**
<ul><li>Cependant</li><li>Néanmoins</li><li>Même si</li><li>Mais</li><li>Pourtant</li><li>Malgré</li><li>En dépit de</li><li>Contrairement</li><li>Tandis que</li><li>D'un autre côté</li><li>Au contraire</li></ul>	<ul><li>De même</li><li>De la même façon</li><li>Comme</li><li>Pareil</li><li>Comparé à</li><li>En comparaison de</li><li>Pas seulement...mais aussi</li></ul>

UNIT 23
PASSIVE

Examples of Passive: « **is made** », « **has been made** », « **will be made** »

The Passive is mostly used in scientific and technical literature and in newspapers but sometimes in conversation as well.

Let's have a quick look at the Passive in English.

What is the difference between:

Paul wrote the report last week.	and	The report was written last week (by Paul).
Paul a écrit le rapport la semaine passée.		Le rapport **a été écrit** (par Paul) la semaine passée.

In the first sentence Paul is the subject and performs the action.

In the second sentence the « report » is the subject but **it does not perform** the action, it is affected by the action, that is why we call it Passive voice.

Les Volvos **sont fabriquées** en Suède. Volvos **are made** in Sweden.

Les billets pour le concert **sont vendus** sur Internet. Tickets for the concert are sold on the Internet.

Cette maison **a été construite** au 19ème siècle. This house was built in 19th century.

The person who performs the action can be introduced by « **par** » or « **de** ».

Shakespeare a écrit Hamlet en 1509. (Active voice)

Shakespeare wrote Hamlet in 1509.

Hamlet, l'une des plus grandes pièces de tous les temps **a été écrite par Shakespeare** en 1509. (Passive voice)

Hamlet, one of the greatest plays of all time, was written by Shakespeare in 1509.

« **Golden** » rule about the Passive:

> **ETRE + participe passé**

This rule has no exceptions. You conjugate the verb **être** in the tense you need and you add the past participle.

Examples with the possible conjugations of ETRE and the past participle of **faire**:

Présent	**est fabriqué** is made / is being made	La Mercedes **est fabriquée** en Allemagne. Mercedes is made in Germany.
Passé composé	**a été fabriqué** was made / has been made	Deux nouveaux modèles **ont été fabriqués** l'année passée. Two new models were made last year.
Imparfait	**était fabriqué** was being made	Le modèle **était déjà fabriqué** quand ils ont décidé de modifier certains détails. The model was being made already when they decided to modify some details.
Plus-que-parfait	**avait été fabriqué** had been made	Ce modèle **avait été fabriqué** avant le lancement de la nouvelle série. This model had been made before the company launched the new series.
Futur simple	**sera fabriqué** will be made	D'autres voitures de ce modèle **seront fabriquées** l'année prochaine. More cars of this model will be made next year.

Futur anterieur	**aura été fabriqué** will have been made	Vers la fin de l'année un grand nombre de voitures de ce modèle **auront été fabriquées.** By the end of the year, a lot of cars of this model will have been made.

EXERCISES — Conjugate the verbs:

1. - Je n'ai pas été ici depuis si longtemps. Je ne savais pas que le pont ... (détruire). I haven't been around for such a long time. I didn't know that the bridge had been destroyed.

- Un nouveau ... (construire) bientôt. A new one will be built soon.

...

2. - Beaucoup de pétards ... (lancer), mais heureusement personne ... (ne pas blesser). A lot of firecrackers were thrown, but fortunately nobody was hurt.

- Je pensais que les pétards ... (interdire) dans les endroits publics. I thought firecrackers were banned in public places.

...

3. - Tu sais que Pit ... (envoyer) au siège à Berlin pour une année ? Do you know that Pit was sent to the headquarters in Berlin for a year?

- Je ... (ne pas savoir). On ... (avoir) besoin d'un autre collègue ici dans ce cas. No, I didn't know. We will need another person here then.

...

4. - Vous avez déjà fini les travaux ? Have you finished the renovation yet?

- Pas encore. L'appartement ...(peindre) déjà, mais la salle de bains ... (rénover). Not yet. The apartment has already been painted, but the bathroom is being renovated now.

ANNEX

ADJECTIVE + PREPOSITION

The preposition can be: **DE, POUR, EN, PAR, A**

→ Gentil(le) **DE** ta part – kind of you

> Merci bien, c'est tellement **gentil de ta part** !
> Thanks a lot, this is so kind of you!

→ Bon(ne) **EN** quelque chose – good at

> Elle est vraiment très **bonne en cuisine**. She is really very good at cooking.

→ Fâché(e) **POUR** quelque chose – angry about something

> Il **se fâche souvent pour de petites choses** au travail.
> He often gets angry about small things at work.

→ Excité(e) / inquiété(e) **PAR** – excited / worried about

> Ils sont très **excités par** leur prochain voyage au Japon.
> They are very excited about their future trip to Japan.

→ Désolé (e)**POUR** / **DE** – sorry to / about

> Je suis **désolé de** vous déranger. I'm sorry to bother you.

→ Fâché(e) **CONTRE** quelqu'un – angry with someone

> **Ne te fâche pas contre moi**, ce n'était pas ma faute.
> Don't be angry with me, it wasn't my fault.

→ Content(e) / satisfait(e) **DE** – pleased / satisfied with

> Je suis **content de** mes progrès en anglais.
> I am satisfied with my progress in English.

→ Déçu(e) **DE** – disappointed with

> Est-ce que **tu es déçue de sa décision ?** Are you disappointed with his decision?

➥ En avoir assez **DE** – to be fed up with

> **J'en ai assez des gens** qui se plaignent tout le temps.
> I'm fed up with people who are complaining all the time.

➥ Surpris(e) **PAR** – surprised by

> Elle était très **surprise par** la nouvelle. She was very surprised by the news.

➥ Effrayé(e) **DE** / avoir peur **DE** – afraid / scared of

> **Je n'ai pas peur des difficultés.** I'm not afraid of difficulties (de +les = des).

➥ Fier(e) **DE** – proud of

> Elle est **fière du succès** de sa fille. She is proud of her daughter's success.

➥ Fatigué(e) **DE** – tired of

> Je suis **fatigué de** travailler beaucoup pour si peu d'argent.
> I'm tired of working hard for little money.

➥ Plein(e) **DE** – full of

> Ce placard **est rempli de** choses inutiles.
> This cupboard is full of useless things.

➥ Connu(e) **POUR** – famous for

> **La France est connue** pour sa cuisine. France is famous for its cuisine.

➥ Responsable **DE** – responsible for

> **Je ne suis pas responsable de** ce désordre.
> I'm not responsible for this mess.

➥ Différent(e) **DE** – different from

> Ce livre est **différent de ce que je m'attendais.**
> The book is different from what I expected.

➥ Similaire **A** – similar to

> Ce plat anglais est **similaire à** notre Hachis Parmentier.
> This English dish is similar to our Hachis Parmentier.

➥ être impressionné(e) **PAR** – be impressed by

> **Nous étions très impressionnés par** le discours du Président.
> We were highly impressed by the President's speech.

➥ Passionné(e) **PAR** – keen on

> Il a toujours été **passionné par le rock**.
> He has always been keen on rock music.

➥ Marié **A** / fiancé **A** – married to / engaged to

> Elle est **mariée à un Italien**. She is married to an Italian.

➥ Amoureux(euse) **DE** – in love with

> Je ne suis pas **amoureuse de lui**, tout simplement il me plaît.
> I'm not in love with him, I just like him.

<u>VERB + PREPOSITION</u>

AUPRES DE, POUR, DE, A, SUR

➥ s'excuser **AUPRES DE** quelqu'un **POUR** quelque chose – to apologize to someone for something

> **Ils se sont excusés auprès des voyageurs** pour le retard.
> They apologized to the travellers for the delay.

➥ se plaindre **AUPRES DE** quelqu'un **DE** quelque chose – to complain **to** someone **about** something

> **Nous nous sommes plaints auprès du** responsable du mauvais service.
> We complained to the manager about the bad service (de + le = du).

➥ penser **A** – to think about

> Il n'y pas besoin de **penser à ce problème**. La solution ne dépend pas de toi.
> There is no good thinking about this problem. The solution doesn't depend on you.

➥ penser **A** (effleurer l'esprit) – to think of

> Dommage que **je n'ai pas pensé à l'appeler** tout de suite.
> Such a pity I didn't think of calling him straight away.

➥ se soucier **DE** – to care about

> **Il ne se soucie pas de** mes problèmes. He doesn't care about my problems.

➥ s'occuper **DE**, prendre soin **DE** – to take care of

> **Je vais m'occuper des fleurs** pendant que tu ne seras pas là.
> I'll take care of the flowers while you are away.

➥ dépendre **DE** – to depend on

> Je veux t'aider, mais **ça ne dépend pas de moi**.
> I want to help you but it doesn't depend on me.

➥ se concentrer **SUR** – to concentrate on

> Tu peux éteindre la musique, s'il te plaît ?
> Je dois me **concentrer sur** mon travail.
> Can you turn off the music, please? I need to concentrate on my work.

➥ dépenser **EN** – to spend on

> A la différence de sa sœur, **elle ne dépense pas beaucoup en** vêtements.
> She doesn't spend much on clothes, unlike her sister.

➥ parler **A / AVEC** – to speak / talk to

> **Je peux parler avec toi** une minute ? Can I talk to you for a minute?

➥ rire **DE** – to laugh at

> **Ne ris pas de moi** ! Ce n'est pas drôle. Don't laugh at me! It's not funny.

➥ crier **SUR** – to shout at

> Ma voisine **crie tout le temps sur ses enfants**.
> Our neighbour is always shouting at her children.

➥ compter **SUR** – to rely on

> Elle est ma meilleure amie, **je peux toujours compter sur elle**.
> She is my best friend, I can always rely on her.

➥ insister **A** – to insist on

> **Le responsable a insisté à prendre** une décision rapide.
> The manager insisted on making a quick decision.

➥ croire **EN** – to believe in

> Tu ne peux pas **croire en Dieu** tant que **tu ne crois pas en toi-même**.
> (proverbe indien) You cannot believe in God until you believe in yourself.

↳ candidater **POUR** un poste – to apply for a job

> J'ai l'intention de **candidater pour ce poste**. I'm going to apply for this job.

↳ faire connaissance **AVEC** – to meet

> **Elle a fait connaissance avec son futur mari** au travail.
> She met her future husband at work.

↳ ne pas avoir assez **DE**, manquer **DE** – to be short of

> **Je manque d'argent** dernièrement. I've been short of money lately.

↳ s'intéresser **A** – be interested in

> La majorité des anglais **s'intéressent au football**.
> Most Englishmen are interested in football.

Between the verb and the preposition there might be an object:

VERB + OBJECT + PREPOSITION

↳ emprunter quelque chose **A** quelqu'un – borrow something from someone

> Je peux **emprunter un peu d'argent à mon frère**.
> I can borrow some money from my brother.

↳ féliciter quelqu'un **POUR** – congratulate someone on

> Je voudrais te **féliciter pour ta nouvelle position** dans l'entreprise !
> I'd like to congratulate you on your new position in the company!

↳ expliquer quelque chose **A** quelqu'un – explain something to someone

> Si tu veux, **je peux t'expliquer les règles de grammaire**. (à toi)
> If you want, I can explain to you the grammar rules.

↳ inviter quelqu'un **A** – invite someone to

> Je vais **inviter beaucoup d'amis à mon anniversaire**.
> I'm going to invite a lot of friends to my Birthday party.

↳ préférer quelque chose **A** quelque chose d'autre – prefer something to something else

> **Je préfère le café au thé**. I prefer coffee to tea.

KEY

Unit 4 ETRE

1. est; n'est-ce pas; n'est pas; 2. es; suis; 3. sont; ne sont pas; sont; 4. es; 5. est; n'est-ce-pas; est

Unit 5 AVOIR

1. as; ai; 2. ai; 3. ai; as; n'est pas; 4. as; avons; 5. a; as; 6. ont; n'ont pas

Unit 9 Pronouns

1. a; les; elle; ils; 2. nos; elle; mon; 3. ma; moi; la; 4. avons; l'; est; 5. les; elle ; 6. ton ; l' ; 7. ta ; l' ; l' ; elle ; 8. mon ; moi ; nos ; nous ; miens ; moi; 9. toi ; le mien

Unit 10 Présent

1. est ce que tu vas; 2. habite; n'est-ce pas; habite; qu'est ce qu'il fait; travaille; est ce qu'il revient; 3. fais; fait; est ce que vous allez; 4. est ce qu'elle habite; elle n'est pas née; est ce qu'elle est née; 5. vous connaissez; 6. fais; vient; 7. sais; sais; 8. vas; 9. essaie; 10. regardes; regarde; j'aime; 11. fais; prépare; 12. n'achète pas; lis; écoute; 13. cherche; préfère; ne vérifies pas; 14. est ce que vous fumez

Unit 12 Prepositions

Mouvement
1. à; 2. à; en; à; 3. à; au; 4. au; à; 5. à; 6. au; 7. sur; 8. à côté; 9. sur; 10. dans

Time
1. en; le; 2. à; 3. de; jusqu'à; 4. – ; 5. à; 6. chez; dans; 7. au; dans

Other prepositions
1. de; 2. de; 3. à; 4. en; à; 5. au; à; jusqu'à; 6. en; en; 7. au ; 8. depuis ; dans ; 9. avec ; de ; de ; 10. entre ; sans ; 11. parmi ; contre ; 12. selon ; à

Unit 13 Adjectives and adverbs

1. tous les; magnifique; 2. exceptionnellement; bonne; 3. plus fort; 4. bien; meilleurs; 5. délicieux; dans le coin; aussi; 6. plus; 7. le plus proche

Unit 14 Passé composé

1. a regardé: ai regardé; 2. avez discuté; avons parlé; 3. n'as pas envoyé; ai oublié; 4. as été; ai été; est allés; 5. as; n'ai pas; ai déjeuné; 6. est arrivé; est resté; 7. as fait; 8. ne l'ai pas vu; n'aime pas; cherche; 9. avez vécu; a été; 10. as écrit; as fait; ai calculé

Unit 15 Imparfait

1. étaient; ont commencé; sont retournés; 2. a plu; ai décidé; ai regretté; était; 3. as acheté, l' ai téléchargé; surfais; ai vu; ai décidé; 4. n'ai pas répondu; parlais; n'as pas rappelé; étais; n'ai pas trouvé; 5. étais; bronzais; étais; étais

Unit 16 Plus-que-parfait

avons eu; faisaient; ont obstrué; a découvert; il y avait; n'avons pas compris; avait commencé; a dû; était; travaillaient; est tombée; n'ont pas pu; sont revenus; se sont rendu compte; avaient oublié; ont dû; a pris; étions restés

Unit 17 Futur

1. vais faire; vais prendre; 2. allons; vont adorer; 3. va avoir; vais appeler; 4. fais; vais le regarder; commence; 5. seront arrivés; vais les appeler; arrive; 6. vais nettoyer; finis; vais t'aider; aurais nettoyé; 7. aura habité

Unit 18 Conditionnel

1. vas venir; suis; n'irai pas; 2. ouvrais; aurais; n'aimais pas; aurais couru; 3. cherche; ne le trouves; vais te donner; 4. étais; candidaterais; était; aurais; 5. ne m'avais pas demandé; serais rentré; 6. ne t'aimait pas; ne t'aurait pas épousée; 7. n'avais menti; aurais

Unit 20 Verbes modaux

1. ne peux pas; dois; dois; 2. peux; pouvons; 3. dois; il ne faut pas; veilles; 4. dois; peux; 5. devraient; 6. ne peux pas; peut; 7. doivent; 8. aurais pas dû; a dû; 9. ai dû; aurais pu

Unit 23 Passive

1. avait été détruit; sera construit; 2. ont été lancés; n'a été blessé; étaient interdits; 3. sera envoyé; ne sais pas; aura; 4. a déjà été; est en train d'être rénovée